Teaching Matters

General Editors: Sydney Hill and Colin

The Sixth Form College in Practice

Peter Watkins

Principal, Price's College, Fareham

Edward Arnold

© Peter Watkins 1982

First published 1982
by Edward Arnold (Publishers) Ltd
41 Bedford Square, London WC1B 3DQ

British Library Cataloguing in Publication Data

Watkins, Peter
    The sixth form college in practice.—(Teaching matters)
    1. Sixth form   2. Education, Secondary—England
    I. Title   II. Series
    373.2'38'0942   LB1620

ISBN 0-7131-0730-8

All Rights Reserved. No part of this publication may be reproduced, stored in a retrieval system, or transmitted in any form or by any means, electronic, mechanical, photocopying, recording or otherwise, without the prior permission of Edward Arnold (Publishers) Ltd.

In-house editor: Gayle Feldman

Text set in 10/11 Baskerville
Printed by Butler & Tanner Ltd, Frome and London

General Editors' Preface

The books in this series provide information and advice on a wide range of educational issues for teachers who are busy, yet who are concerned to keep abreast of new developments.

The aim is practicality: slim volumes that are sources of authoritative help and swift reference, written and edited by people whose expertise in their field is backed up by experience of the everyday realities of school and classroom. The books are planned to cover well-defined topics relevant to schools in widely differing situations: subject teaching, curriculum development, areas of responsibility within schools, and the relationship of the school to the community. They are published at a time when there is a growing call for increased professional accountability in our primary and secondary schools. The 'in-service between covers' that characterizes these handbooks is designed to contribute to the vitality and development of schools and of the individuals within them.

The author of this book has had experience of very different sorts of school. In recent years he has been in turn the head of a voluntary aided city grammar school and of an 11–18 comprehensive before becoming principal of one of the largest sixth form colleges in the country. His personal experience is here backed up with abundant evidence he has collected of the wide variety of practice in the first 100 sixth form colleges to be set up in England and Wales. The opportunities and problems encountered by the staff and students of these new institutions are shrewdly analysed. There is also much on the curriculum, timetable, and pastoral organization that will be of relevance to all dealing with the age group, whether they are school or college based.

During the next few years many more colleges are likely to be established as authorities seek to reorganize the education of 16–19 year olds at a time of falling rolls and scarce resources. This book will therefore be of immediate practical interest to many besides teachers. Governors, administrators, parents—even some of the students themselves—will find it an authoritative, judicious and highly readable guide.

Foreword

I wish to record my gratitude to friends and colleagues who have provided me with their college brochures and much other information, administered questionnaires and allowed me to visit their colleges. These, together with the publications of the Association of Principals of Sixth Form Colleges, have provided information without which I could not have claimed to generalize, as I have done, about the practices of sixth form colleges. I am particularly grateful to Mr John Glazier, Principal of South East Essex Sixth Form College, who read my first draft and made many valuable suggestions for improvement.

This brief guide to sixth form colleges is precisely what its title suggests: an attempt to describe the colleges as they are. It is neither an apologia nor a polemic. I hold the view that 16–19 education in the 1980s is far too complex an issue and is changing far too rapidly to be susceptible to any single or simple solution. That sixth form colleges work, I am convinced, and that they are making a valuable contribution to the education of the age group, I have no doubt.

January 1982   PRW

Contents

1 From sixth form to sixth form college
Introduction 1
The roots of the sixth form 1
The grammar school sixth form 2
The comprehensive sixth form 3
The origins of the sixth form college 4
The first sixth form colleges 5
Developments since 1966 7

2 The nature of the college
Provision for the 16–19 age group 9
Open access 10
The break at sixteen 12
Categories of student 15
The aims of the college 17
Buildings 18

3 Management and staffing
Principal and vice-principals 21
Faculties or departments 22
Pastoral organization 24
The group tutor 25
Deployment of staff 28
Staff experience of the college 30

4 Curriculum and examinations
Curriculum constraints: GCE A & O level 32
Advanced level 35
Ordinary level 37
Curriculum considerations: other courses 38
CEE and CSE 40
Pre-vocational courses 41
Foundation courses 45

5 Curriculum and general education
The problem of general education	47
General education as the core of the curriculum	50
General education through an examined course for all	51
General education through modular courses	52
Learning to learn	52
Religious education	55
Careers education and work experience	56

6 The college programme
The framework of the day	58
The box structure	64
The student programme	70
The college meeting	72
Work assignments	73
Rules and sanctions	75
The student council	77

7 From school to college
The short course comprehensive school	78
Liaison between school and college	80
Admission and induction	83
Collaboration with further education	86

8 The student view
Student expectations	89
Settling down and making friends	90
The academic programme	92
Rules and sanctions	94
A student view of the sixth form college	96

9 Conclusion
99

References and bibliography
103

1

From sixth form to sixth form college

Introduction

Like the era of the cowboys and Indians in the history of the United States, the classic grammar school sixth form combines a brief golden age with a profound and lasting mythology. As a numerically significant feature of the state system of education, the grammar school sixth form was the creation of the years after the Second World War. From 1965 onwards it was increasingly under threat, as comprehensive reorganization swept the country and the debate on 16-19 provision got under way. There have emerged a variety of ways of providing for the needs of those requiring full-time education beyond 16, and among them the sixth form college has proved increasingly popular. By 1981 there were 102 colleges, providing for about 60,000 students, over 18% of all sixth formers.

The roots of the sixth form

The term sixth form appears to have originated at Winchester where, in the seventeenth century, the college was divided into seven classes or books, of which one dropped out leaving the sixth as the top form**(45)**. By no means all schools used the term. As late as 1910 King Edward's School, Birmingham, since the 1840's one of the outstanding academic schools of the country, referred to the top form taught by the headmaster as the First class, a practice followed in the new grammar schools originating in the 1880's from the same foundation. Content is, however, more important than nomenclature. The sixth form became identified in the nineteenth century with academic learning and close connections with the ancient universities but it was also concerned with character training and social responsibility, ideals encapsulated in the phrase 'godliness and good learning'.

From the public schools and the great city grammar schools, the sixth form tradition passed into the new local authority grammar schools, founded under the impulse of the Balfour Act of 1902 and according to the model of Sir Robert Morant. It was, however, only a tiny elite which constituted the sixth form of those days. Of 16 and 17 year olds, one per cent in 1894, according to the Bryce Commission, and a mere two per cent, according to the 1911 census, were to be found in school**(15)**.

Specialization in a group of related subjects was the contribution of the Higher School Certificate, begun in 1917 to eliminate the chaos of existing examinations, and so the Science and the Arts Sixth took their place alongside the Classical Sixth. The regulations requiring specialization lasted until 1937 but by then the pattern had been established and the practice persisted. There was growth in the inter-war years: numbers doubled between 1926 and 1937, but reached only 40,000 or about seven per cent of the age group and were doing no more than reflect the expansion of secondary education as a whole. A peak was reached in 1932 and the late 1930's saw a decline. Before the Second World War the average size of a grammar school sixth form was under twenty and few exceeded fifty. Some of those who stayed on did so only for one year, to turn a School Certificate into matriculation exemption in order to enter the local civic university. Private study made its appearance arising from the impossibility of staffing small subject groups, rather than from any theory about the value of independent work.

The grammar school sixth form

It was the post-war years which saw the brief flourishing of the classic grammar school sixth form, regarded today with nostalgia by a generation now middle aged, who were its first beneficiaries. Schools Council Working Paper Number 5 rightly described the sixth form as 'a subgroup which often constitutes a society in its own right'. Transition from fifth form to sixth form, unlike that from tenth to eleventh grade in an American senior high school, was never a natural progression. It was an entrée to a new world, a world of privilege, private study, prefectship and specialization. The atmosphere was that of an elite. Entrance depended on two criteria. One was academic, usually the achievement of five Ordinary level passes, in 'established academic subjects', meant to exclude such dubious 'soft options' as art, woodwork and home economics. The second criterion was harder to define: 'suitability' is perhaps the best blanket term. It involved an attitude to work and to the school as a whole, the likelihood of co-operative relations with staff, 'the right attitude' and the ability to benefit from the ambience of the sixth form. Hence the emergence of that interesting hybrid 5Ex or the General VI, whose academic inadequacy was compounded by doubtful attitudes and who needed a further year to O level. The full privileges of the sixth form were either withheld altogether or conceded only grudgingly. Hence, too, the reluctance of schools to take the opportunity to by-pass O level, when School and Higher School Certificates were replaced by the GCE. By so doing the distinction between fifth and sixth form would have been unacceptably blurred.

The sixth form grew, with the years after 1955 seeing the most spectacular increase. The full employment of those halcyon years placed a premium on better qualifications, which in turn was both cause and effect of the equally spectacular explosion of higher education. A higher proportion of jobs were professional and managerial, while the emancipation of women increased the number of girls entering the sixth form. The Crowther Report of 1959 recorded the average size of a sixth form as 41 in 1952, 65 in 1959 and expected it to reach 98 by 1966. It was the sixth form of the late 1950's that the report describes in such reverential tones. It rightly pointed out that the only schools which as yet made any appreciable numerical contribution to sixth form education were maintained and direct grant grammar schools and independent schools. It described the five marks of the sixth form: close links with the university, 'subject-mindedness' (a special devotion to a particular branch of study), independent work, 'intellectual discipleship' and social responsibility.

A sixth form tradition of this sort was the aspiration of grammar schools old and new which flourished in the quarter of a century after the Second World War. It commanded the loyalty of the staff and in varying degrees of those educated within it, though it must be conceded that it was more characteristic of boys' grammar schools than of either girls' or mixed grammar schools. When comprehensive reorganization came, it was the dilution or disappearance of the sixth form which provoked most reasoned opposition.

The comprehensive sixth form

When, in the post-war years, the pioneer comprehensive schools were being planned by authorities such as Bristol, Coventry and the ILEA, one of the main questions was how large the school needed to be if the sixth form were to offer the variety of A level subjects and the educational experience available in the grammar school sixth form. It was to support such a sixth form that the early comprehensive schools were planned to accommodate up to 2000 pupils, though later this was reduced to 1500. It was out of concern that such schools might prove unwieldy or impersonal and the belief that adequate A level provision required a sixth form of 120, that the tiered school was born. Leicestershire was the pioneer, opening its first high schools for the 13/14–18 age group at Wigston and Hinckley in 1957(**32**).

There have continued to be nagging doubts about the minimum size of sixth form which is both cost-effective and educationally stimulating. Estimates vary from 80–140. The average size of school sixth form grew from 72 to 80 between 1967 and 1979, but almost one quarter of sixth forms numbered under 50 in 1979. One aspect which has perhaps been insufficiently stressed is the proportion of the total school population which is represented by the sixth form. A three form entry grammar school may produce a sixth form of 130, all taking A level and this will constitute 22% of the school. An eight form entry comprehensive school enerates a sixth form of the same size, but this will constitute less than 10% of the school population and not all will be taking A level. The difference lies in the smaller proportion of staff time and energy which can be devoted to the sixth form, and the smaller impact its members can be expected to have on the life of the school.

Size, however, is only one facet of the comprehensive sixth form. Its early supporters were out to prove that it could compete with the grammar school on its own terms: for places in higher education, including Oxford and Cambridge, for A level results, football fixtures and sixth form conferences. It soon became clear that the grammar school sixth form with its highly selective entry was alien to the philosophy of comprehensive education. After all, was a 16+ hurdle all that much better than an 11+ examination? And so the open sixth was born and the new sixth former entered it. The 5Ex pupil of the grammar school was now welcome as a one year sixth former converting his CSE to O level or, after 1972, taking the pilot CEE examinations. And where the comprehensive school led, the grammar school followed. In 1974, 71% of comprehensive schools had an open sixth, while 25% of independent and direct grant schools had moved in that direction, as had 30% of boys' maintained grammar schools(**45**). The two sectors influenced each other. The comprehensive schools strove for the conventional academic prowess of the grammar schools, which in their turn became less elitist. Their prefect systems became more democratic, their dress regulations were relaxed, streaming was ended and express routes to the sixth form were phased out.

The origins of the sixth form college

The idea of the sixth form college occurred to Rupert Wearing King shortly before the Second World War. In 1954, now Chief Education Officer for Croydon, he found a borough with five grammar schools whose sixth forms totalled 269, three of them with under 50 in each. If economy were to be the sole criterion, the subject take-up in the five schools provided an unanswerable case for his scheme for Addington College, his prototype sixth form college. The grammar school heads and staffs banded together in opposition and the scheme was defeated. Far more than economy of provision was at stake; the issue was nothing less than the nature of a grammar school. If a nineteenth century public school without a chapel could be described as an angel without wings, the same could surely be said of a twentieth century grammar school without a sixth form. King remained, however, an advocate of the sixth form college and the envoi of his book published in 1968 described it as 'the only way'(**29**).

Another early protagonist was William Alexander who, as Director of Education for Sheffield from 1939-1944, recommended centralized sixth form provision for the post-war city. It was, however, Sir Geoffrey Crowther who was the first advocate of the 'open access' sixth form or junior college. He recalled how, when his report was being prepared, the idea encountered the opposition of all but one of his professional colleagues and he was allowed 'an anodyne reference to the possibility of experiments in this field as a concession to the foibles of the chairman'. He saw the junior college, standing alongside the sixth form, 'providing an alternative form of education for those who had got incurably tired of school or for those whose schools had no sixth form', 'an institution emancipated from memories of childhood and tutelage'. 'We are not of course sure', the report continued, 'that there is room for such an institution in the English educational system, it would be impossible to be sure without a trial ... We would welcome experiments'**(29, 6)**.

As a practical proposition the sixth form college is the consequence of Circular 10/65 issued by Anthony Crosland during his brief period as Secretary of State for Education and Science. Intent by now on speeding up the progress of comprehensive reorganization and needing to circumvent the argument that without new buildings change was impossible, the Circular listed six alternative ways of going comprehensive. The fifth alternative was '(a) 11–16 schools followed by a sixth form college or (b) 11–16 schools co-existing with 11–18 schools, the latter providing the sixth form'. The merits of 11–18 schools were, however, stressed. The 11–16 school, it concluded, 'has at first sight few arguments to commend it', while sixth form colleges were referred to as 'experiments', of which only a limited number would be allowed. The circular clearly anticipated two kinds of college, one with restricted entry providing academic education, and the other with no entry bar, catering for the needs of all students in the 16–19 age group who wanted full time education. Both models were soon to have their prototypes and it looked at first sight as though authorities contemplating a break at 16 might opt for one or the other.

The first sixth form colleges

The first schools providing exclusively for those of sixth form age were outside the maintained system. Welbeck College was opened in 1953 by the army to provide for boys going on to Sandhurst to train for a career in its technical corps. Atlantic College opened in 1962 with the intention of providing an international education with an outdoor and community emphasis. From the beginning it stressed an all-round education and pioneered the International Baccalaureate. Curiously neither has exercised much influence on the state system, perhaps because they serve a specialized function and are both highly selective.

The title of the first sixth form college was claimed by George Shield, its headmaster, for Mexborough Sixth Form College which opened in 1964. It was, however, in current parlance, a sixth form centre, a 'mushroom' institution drawing students not only from the fifth form of Mexborough Grammar School with whom it shared site, staff and facilities, but also from local secondary modern schools. Rosebery Grammar School for Girls at Epsom was another example of such a 'mushroom'.

It was the newly formed county borough of Luton which provided the first operational sixth form college. The authority planned in the mid-sixties two colleges, each to provide advanced academic education of sixth form standard. The DES modified the scheme, authorizing only one college and requiring more flexible entrance requirements than the four O levels proposed in the submission. The criterion remained, however, that entrants should be capable of a course with some A level content(**9**). The college opened in September 1966. Staff at Luton wrote a preparatory paper entitled 'Vision of a Sixth Form College', expressing the hope that it might be 'something between a school and a university, maybe more akin to a modern teacher training college', and referred to 'this fascinating experiment in sixth form living' (**3**). In 1971 Luton broadened its entry policy further and it became possible to take O level courses.

If Luton in its early days was the prototype of the academic sixth form college, then Southampton, also at that time a small county borough, though incorporated in Hampshire in 1974, was the pioneer of the open access college. In 1967 three of the city's grammar schools were designated secondary colleges. Itchen Grammar School became a co-educational college while Taunton's School and Southampton College for Girls provided, respectively, a college for boys and one for girls. They remained for a decade the only single sex sixth form colleges. In the late 1970's both became co-educational, the erstwhile girls' college renamed Hill College. The published history of Taunton's School is a reminder that reorganization to become a sixth form college could be every bit as unacceptable as the apparently more drastic change from grammar school to comprehensive school. The writer recalls the eloquent and bitter attack launched on the authority's scheme at the last Speech Day in 1966 held in the Southampton Guildhall. The headmaster, R. P. Challacombe, described the 'wanton destruction' as he saw it, of two hundred years of tradition and achievement just when the school appeared to be at its peak(**43**).

Most sixth form colleges are adaptations of buildings provided for other purposes, usually grammar schools. It was Stoke-on-Trent, yet another small county borough, which provided the first purpose built college. Since 1963, Longton High School had provided an embryo college by transfer of 16 year olds from six junior high schools and by 1969 there were 400 in the sixth form(**9**). In September 1970, the City of Stoke Sixth Form College began, 'designed specifically for young adults preparing for universities and colleges'. It had been formally opened on 10 April 1970 by the then Prime Minister, Harold Wilson.

Developments since 1966

The movement towards sixth form colleges which had begun in the late 1960's gathered momentum in the early 1970's. Fifteen colleges were designated to open in 1973 and another 21 in 1974. Thereafter the pace slackened, but in 1980 the total in existence reached one hundred. It seems likely that there will be a further boom in the mid-1980's as local authorities reconsider 16-19 provision in response to falling rolls and the need for economy. The peak years for the sixth form cohort were 1981-1982 while the trough will occur in 1993-1994, though there are substantial regional and local variations of both scale and timing(**23**).

Only rarely have sixth form colleges been provided for a whole county. Bury, Harrow, Salford and Tameside are the only authorities whose maintained sixth form provision is wholly in sixth form colleges and Richmond-on-Thames the only one whose provision is wholly in a tertiary college. In Hampshire, which has 12 sixth form colleges and at Andover the first purpose built tertiary college in the country, 11/12-18 schools are to be found in Gosport and Portsmouth and in the south-east and north-east of the county. Sixth form colleges have sometimes provided a means of retaining the identity of a prestigious voluntary aided school such as Collyer's School in Horsham, West Sussex or King Edward VI School, Stourbridge. Sixth form colleges have proved popular with Roman Catholic school authorities. Cities like Birmingham, Bristol and Manchester, whose local authority provision is at present in 11-18 schools, all provide examples of sixth form colleges for the Catholic section of the school population.

The size of sixth form colleges varies greatly, averaging 569 in January 1981. The largest colleges including Luton, Stoke-on-Trent and South

The development of sixth form colleges 1966-1981

Year	Number opened	Total	Year	Number opened	Total
1966	1	1	1974[1]	21	57
1967	4	5	1975	10	67
1968	1	6	1976	9	76
1969	4	10	1977[2]	8	81
1970	3	13	1978	6	87
1971	1	14	1979	10	97
1972	8	22	1980	4	101
1973	15	37	1981	1	102

[1] Preston, opened in 1969 as a sixth form college, was reorganized as W. R. Tuson College (tertiary) in 1974.
[2] Thames Valley College and Shene College were opened in 1973 as sixth form colleges and were replaced by Richmond-upon-Thames College (tertiary) in 1977. King James' College, Huddersfield was opened in 1974 and closed in 1977.

East Essex, all approach 1200. Bilston Sixth Form College, Wolverhampton with 109 students was the smallest. A further five colleges have around 300 students.

There is usually a time lag of five years between the designation of a college and its providing solely for the 16–19 age group. Of the 101 colleges in 44 authorities in January 1981, 81 were providing exclusively for the 16–19 age group while the remainder were in transition.

2

The nature of the college

Provision for the 16–19 age group

Like the European middle ages, the 16–19 age group owes its definition to what lies on either side of it. It is neither childhood nor adulthood. Parental controls are loosened but not dissolved, and the requirement of compulsory schooling is over. On the other hand, full citizenship is withheld. In matters such as voting, sexual behaviour, driving a car and purchasing alcohol, most of the age group to be found in the sixth form college is not adult. No satisfactory word has yet been coined to describe their place in education. The Crowther Report of 1959 was called simply, '15 to 18' and the Macfarlane Report of 1980 followed this example with '16 to 19'. For a time it seemed that the term 'tertiary' might become a suitable omnibus expression, but it is now too late; one type of post-16 institution has pre-empted the term. 'Tertiary systems', however, is used increasingly to indicate the variety of provision for the 16–19 age group, overlapping the school and further education sectors.

Four types of institution cater for those wishing to continue in full-time education beyond 16. The traditional providers, school sixth forms and technical or further education colleges, are now supplemented by two newcomers to the scene, tertiary colleges and sixth form colleges. The first tertiary college was Exeter College, opened in 1970, and there are now sixteen of them. They combine the secondary school sixth form and the further education college in a single institution, run under Further Education regulations. They provide full-time academic, general and vocational education alongside part-time day and evening courses and claim to represent a synthesis of the best in the school and further education traditions. Most tertiary colleges have upwards of 1000 full-time students, though Strode College, Street is an exception with 400 full-time students(**27, 44**).

The sixth form college is to many people the sixth form writ large. Like its precursor it provides a full-time, academic and liberal education through a subject based curriculum within a community, membership of which is involuntary and intangible. There are, however, three factors which at once differentiate the college from the school sixth form: the narrow age range, the short stay of the students and the scale of the institution. The absence of younger pupils intensifies peer group identification, while in large numbers the age group can prove less biddable than the smaller sixth form. A sense of community is intuitive and of slow growth and the short stay of the students inhibits its development. There are, however, gains. There is a premium on settling down quickly, and virtue in the brevity and intensity of the college experience. The short stay brings greater stress on instrumental goals. Students do not join the college football team or act in the college play because they enjoyed the comradeship of the under 15 team last year, or out of loyalty to the college, but because they like football or acting. The scale of the institution brings changes, too. Five physics sets may mean greater professionalism in the teaching but A level physicists may not feel part of a scientific elite as they might in the school sixth form. None of these factors is a dramatic break with the past. Taken together they accentuate developments which have been going on for some time. Sixth form blocks, isolated from the main school, cast doubts on the claim that close contact between sixth formers and younger pupils is essential to their mutual well-being. Sixth form colleges can develop an identity which includes a more relaxed style and a more mature version of the philosophy which has been exemplified in the sixth form of the recent past.

Open access

The early colleges saw themselves as exemplars of one of two models, which appeared at first to be sharply differentiated. The colleges at Luton and Stoke were characterized by an entry bar and academic orientation. The Southampton colleges, on the other hand, were described as secondary colleges. In the first *Compendium of Sixth Form and Tertiary Colleges* (1974), the colleges in Harrow were described as junior colleges and Havant appeared as Havant Comprehensive College**(44)**. According to Benn and Simon (1972), the selective college was designed specifically to act as a high powered grammar school**(2)**. David Carter, a member of the staff at Luton, described it as a 'Noah's ark to carry traditional academic values over the floodtide of declining standards'**(4)**. There was a suggestion that here were two philosophies, one meritocratic, substituting a 16+ for an 11+, and the other egalitarian, a genuine completion of a comprehensive system of education.

In fact the picture is much more complex than this. The title sixth form college is now almost universal. This is not because the academic model has won the day, rather the opposite. No college feels it necessary to adopt a title which proclaims its comprehensive nature because almost all now see themselves as part of a comprehensive system of education. In theory at least, open access has triumphed. In the *Compendium of Sixth Form and Tertiary Colleges* (1982), only Solihull S.F. College and the two Cambridge colleges admit to an entry bar, though King

George V College, Southport and Hereford S.F. College are silent on the subject. Solihull S.F. College 'draws its strength from the grammar school tradition' and requires five O level passes to ensure admission. All the remaining colleges claim to be open access. 'Open access' refers to the willingness of the college to admit students without academic entry requirements. The corollary of this is that there are courses for the needs of the whole ability range, from candidates for Oxford and Cambridge to the educationally subnormal. This is, however, not always the case for two reasons. First, a substantial proportion of the age group do not currently participate in full-time education post-16, nor is it likely that they would do so merely because appropriate courses were provided. With rising youth unemployment many sixth form colleges are extending their range of provision to meet the new need. Second, there may be a deliberate policy by either the local authority or the college to avoid overlapping provision. Technical colleges provide vocational courses of which A level is a component and they may be more suitable for some students than an A level course in the sixth form college. A long tradition, suitable plant and equipment and a desire for economy may determine the demarcation between two colleges by policy or mutual agreement. There is likely in the future to be increasing co-operation between sixth form and technical colleges to provide lower level courses with differing emphasis for the young unemployed. The problem of overlap, however, is a complex one. Some governing bodies demand that the sixth form college shall be open access but that there shall be no overlapping provision. In fact the less overlapping there is, the likelier it will be that the sixth form college will in practice have a heavy bias towards GCE courses and the technical college will provide vocationally oriented courses. There are, of course, areas where two or more sixth form and further education colleges are in competition with one another. Courses may then be provided in a deliberate attempt to attract students to a given college.

The image of the institution may influence demand, particularly in the early years of the college. The former grammar school may retain an aura of academic selectivity and so encourage the contributory schools to recommend its average or below average students to go to the technical college. In another area the former grammar school may appeal to parents who see lower level courses acquiring a cachet through being offered at a prestigious institution.

The result is a highly complex picture. It is, however, clear that no hard and fast line can be drawn between the selective and the open access college. There is instead a continuum, which can best be measured by the proportion of sixth formers to be found in any given college who are taking no A level subjects. At one end stand Solihull S.F. College, King George V College, Southport, Hereford S.F. College and King Edward VI College, Nuneaton, where the sixth form college caters solely for A level candidates. At the other end West Park College, Sandwell has 45% of its students on non-A level courses. In the Southampton colleges non-A level sixth formers average 30%. The average of non-A level sixth formers countrywide is 21%, remarkably close to the average for all schools and colleges.

Open access, however, is not simply a statement about admission policy or the provision of courses, but an attitude of mind and an approach to student needs. The traditional grammar school sixth form was concerned with providing a specialist education for the able minority. It was deliberately exclusive, resistant to outside influences and hesitant in the face of innovation. The open access college questions all these assumptions. It seeks a broader spectrum of students and sets out to provide for their needs. It values all its students equally, whether they are taking A level or a City and Guilds Foundation course. It encourages contacts with other forms of 16–19 education, with industry and with the outside world. It positively favours innovation. Freed from the pressures involved in dealing with younger adolescents, the staff of a sixth form college is concerned to explore new strategies for gaining knowledge and applying it to new situations. In reply to a questionnaire about the staff experience of working in a sixth form college, one recently appointed teacher complained that there was inadequate opportunity on the form to convey the sheer exhilaration of working in an institution emancipated from so many of the constraints which have prevented the school sixth form being the exciting educational experience which it ought to be. The task of the college is to draw all its students into a common educational experience relevant to their individual needs.

The break at sixteen

There is no conclusive evidence on educational grounds for or against a break at sixteen. It seems, however, that under the circumstances of the 1980's economic and pragmatic arguments will tend to favour separate provision for the post-16 age group. What is more, some of the arguments which have appeared to favour continuity have a reverse side to them.

The needs of schools and their pupils

The existence of a sixth form in an 11–18 comprehensive school has, it is claimed, an effect on the total life of the school, influencing it for good both as an academic and as a social institution. From the age of about 14, pupils become increasingly aware of their seniors in the sixth form. They are influenced by the knowledge that whatever course they choose, there are others ahead of them on the same route, guided by the same staff who are teaching them. Sixth formers set standards of behaviour, captain the football and cricket teams, play in the orchestra and take the lead in the school play. In countless ways the sixth form provides the models needed by younger pupils as they go through the difficult adolescent years, while the sixth formers themselves gain a sense of responsibility and opportunities for leadership which contribute intangibly to their own education.

This is, however, a one-sided view. On the academic side some quite able fifth formers react against the automatic assumption that they will follow the same well trodden route as their predecessors. For others a school subject has become too exclusively associated with the personality of a given member of the staff and needs now to be viewed objectively before being selected for sixth form study. For the less able, the sixth form may appear to be an alien existence and its academic pace-setters people with whom they cannot identify. On the social side it is valuable for fifth formers in their last year of compulsory schooling to have the experience of leadership and the exercise of responsibility, an opportunity available thereby to all, not just those who will continue in full-time education beyond 16. The work of Michael Rutter et al. suggested that both behaviour and examination results were better when a high proportion of pupils held positions of responsibility(**34**). Certainly the fifth formers who come for interview at the sixth form college, with prefect badges on their blazers and team captaincies listed on their application forms, appear to have appreciated the opportunities they have received. For many schools the transition period of losing a sixth form may be traumatic; the experience of normal life without one is usually very satisfying.

The needs of the sixteen year old
It has been argued, secondly, that it is precisely those students who have experienced greatest difficulty at school who will suffer most severely from the dislocation of their education at 16. In the absence of a stable home background, some have established a relationship with particular members of staff. Others have learning difficulties or emotional problems which are understood by a house or year head who has followed their progress through four or five years of secondary schooling. Those from limited backgrounds, it was thought, would be more likely to enter the sixth form of their own school than to make the transition to a wholly new environment.

These assumptions too, have their reverse side. Some who have benefited most from the emotional support of school are ready at 16 to move on. Some prefer their juvenile indiscretions or even crimes, to be forgotten; others that the traumatic circumstances surrounding a divorce or a death in the family should not always be remembered. The class buffoon is glad to establish a different persona in new surroundings. Even for the more timid, the temporary pain of parting with familiar faces and places is necessary for maturation. Staying-on rates have risen whenever post-16 provision has been in sixth form colleges. Between 1967 and 1977 the number in the three colleges in Southampton almost trebled from

650–1700, with only a small proportion attributable to an increase in the age group.

It is over twenty years ago since the Crowther Report noted that 'the presence of quite young boys and girls involves paternalistic discipline which quite often spreads upwards to those who do not need it'. In the ensuing decades schools, as a result of wider social changes, have become less paternalistic but this in turn has been balanced by the greater maturity of the 16 year old and the danger remains as great as it was when Crowther wrote. The Schools Council Sixth Form Survey (1970) showed the developing demand among pupils of 16 for an ethos, atmosphere and attitude which were different from those of school, a view confirmed in the late 1970's by the work of Dean, Bradley et al**(31, 10)**. Many sixth formers at best tolerate what they still regard as the paternalism of school. In many places prefect systems have melted in the noon-day sun, their duties regarded as trivial and burdensome, their privileged status unwanted and their elitist assumptions unacceptable. Whatever schools may feel about the advantages of contact with younger pupils, it is not a view widely shared by the young people themselves. The strongest argument for the sixth form college is the opportunity to provide an institution suited to the needs of an age group which looks naturally forward to adult models.

The needs of staff

Many people have argued that the most serious effect of a break in education at 16 is on the recruitment, promotion and job satisfaction of the teaching profession. The opportunity to teach sixth form pupils for A level, the argument runs, attracts highly qualified staff. It provides an incentive for maintaining academic interests and so continues within the mainstream of compulsory schooling the tradition of teaching as a learned profession. The proportion, however, of most teachers' timetables which is likely to be made up by A level work will be small, scarcely enough to provide time or incentive for the necessary reading and preparation. Just how many teachers are there who can do justice to pupils ranging in age from 11 to 18 and in ability from slow learners to university aspirants? How many can turn easily from the latest article in *The Economic History Review* to prepare a plaster model of a medieval castle for the second form? There are without doubt some able teachers who possess the versatility and value the variety of stimulus; they are probably a minority. More find that the strain of teaching in a comprehensive school is in part the result of attempting to cope with such conflicting demands. Under such circumstances it may be the demanding academic preparation for good sixth form teaching which suffers.

Promotion in the profession, too, may be easier, not harder, where there is a break at 16. For the post of head of department in an 11–16 school, likely to be at Scale 3 or 4, there will be a premium on the gifted teacher with all-round expertise with the age group, and no need to recruit an academic who can teach the sixth form.

Categories of student

When Crowther turned in part five of his report to the sixth form, he entitled the first chapter 'The Ablest Boys and Girls'. It was for these that the sixth form was designed and for them that the normal academic A level course was appropriate. Only at the end of the section in a chapter entitled 'Sixth Forms With a Difference', did he discuss 'courses which are not linked with university entrance requirements', and in particular the provision in girls' schools of general courses lasting one year, providing a preparation for professions such as teaching and nursing. The report suggested that there was scope for general courses for boys, too, but the author was not sure whether they should be provided in schools or in other institutions.

Twenty years on from Crowther the situation is much more complex. The Macfarlane Report of 1980, surveying the educational needs of the 16–19 age group, identified seven broad categories (paragraph 29, my italics):

A those who enter *employment* and receive *no structured part-time education or training*

B those who enter *employment* and who have the opportunity for *systematic education and training* leading normally to an educational, vocational or professional qualification

C those *without work* or immediate prospects of work

These three groups do not continue in full-time education, though some who might otherwise be in group **C**, may in present circumstances do so.

D those staying [in education] with a view to proceeding to *higher education* in due course

E those seeking an essentially *vocational qualification* to fit them to enter employment at some stage up to 18

F those who do not wish to be committed to a specific vocational objective, but who wish to continue their *general education, personal development and pre-employment preparation*

G those who require *remedial education* to enhance their employment and life prospects

Group **D** was Crowther's sixth form and is still a large component of all sixth forms and sixth form colleges. Some of group **D**, however, are to be found in further education taking A level, sometimes alongside vocational courses and destined subsequently for higher education, perhaps on a sandwich course. 11% of A level students are now found in FE colleges. Some, in both sixth form and further education colleges, have come from the independent sector whose life-style, single sex regime or fees the students themselves or their parents have found uncongenial. Some parents deliberately choose independent schools up to 16, but are then pleased for their children to enter a maintained sixth form college. About 10% of entrants to sixth form colleges come from independent schools, though the proportion varies a great deal according to area. The group heading for higher education is itself a varied one. Some are academic high fliers with strong motivation and a good measure of disinterested intellectual curiosity; they are destined to be the original thinkers, the leaders of the professions and the captains of industry in the next generation. Sixth form college students now figure prominently among entrants to Oxford and Cambridge, having taken 98 open awards in December 1980. Others are sustained through an academic course by strong career motivation towards engineering, law or medicine, for example, for which good A level grades are essential

On the borderline between Macfarlane's groups **D** and **F**, come A level candidates, who have no clear view of the future and who, on entering the college, have no destination in mind. Some are able and motivated generally, some are able but unmotivated, while some will struggle throughout the course and be among the 35% who obtain not more than one pass grade at A level. They form a significant group, whose need for pastoral care and careers education in its broadest sense is paramount. They are also the A level candidates most likely to drop out. About 12% of those who embark on a two year A level programme do not reach the second year of the course.

Group **E** is found predominantly in technical colleges, preparing in Macfarlane's words, 'for work in catering, hairdressing, community fields and secretarial jobs', the vocational content of their course providing also the means of their general education. A few sixth form colleges, mainly those situated at a distance from a technical college, offer vocational courses which meet the needs of this group. Many offer secretarial courses taken up mostly by girls, and also offer City and Guilds Foundation courses.

Group **F**, those 'who wish to continue their general education, personal development and pre-employment preparation', is the second major concern of the school sixth form and sixth form college. For some the sixth form year is a remedial one, repeating qualifications which they failed to obtain a year earlier. For some, whose development has been slower, this is a genuine sixth year, to complete what abler pupils have achieved in five years. Many are well motivated, respond to the new institution and not only succeed in their one year course, but then embark on a two or three A level course in the college and some subsequently take a degree course. Some, however, will neither retrieve past failure— they have already reached a plateau—nor achieve in a sixth year what others have achieved in five. It is for these that CEE (Certificate of Extended Education) has proved to be a major course component. Macfarlane, following the government's consultative paper, *Examinations 16–18*, recommends for these an entirely new course model, a pre-vocational one along the lines of the FECRDU report *A Basis for Choice*(**13, 16**).

The Warnock Report placed emphasis on the provision of post-16 education for Macfarlane's group **G**, those with special educational needs. There are a number of overlapping categories. Some are too personally immature or insecure to seek or hold a job. Others still need to achieve adequate standards of numeracy and literacy and to acquire further life skills. For these students, provision may be available in either further education or in schools. The sixth form college, with its community life and well developed pastoral system, is well suited to meet their needs.

Any categorization of students involves over-simplification. There is a continuum of ability and motivation, and an infinite variety of individual need. Sixth form colleges take a high proportion of students destined for higher education but in recent years there has been a substantial increase in the number of students of average ability in the colleges, and much curriculum development has taken place to meet this need. One of the major themes of the Macfarlane Report was that 16–19 education needed to be viewed as a whole, with less emphasis than in the past on the sectoral divisions between schools and FE. It seems likely that there will be a further blurring of the distinction between the sectors, as both seek to provide for the age group.

The aims of the college

It is not easy for a new institution to establish its own identity. It is more likely to acquire it by accident or association, by contrast with other institutions or by definition from the public. Comprehensive schools and sixth form colleges have both in the last 20 years faced all these hazards. Sixth form colleges have the disadvantage of a name which is heavily allusive and in some ways misleading. They are associated in the public mind with grammar schools and by contrast with technical colleges. It has been easier for new purpose-built colleges to establish their own identity than it has for 'conversion' colleges to do so. The latter are often associated with the institution whose buildings they inherited, or contrasted with the sixth form of a nearby ex-direct grant grammar school.

Sixth form colleges have grown up within the school tradition of education, with its Christian, liberal and humanist assumptions. They have a role in loco parentis even if the courts have never been asked to decide what this means post-16. They set out to educate the whole person and contribute to moral and spiritual, as well as mental and physical, development. They provide games, art, music and drama. They are educating not just tomorrow's employers and employees but also tomorrow's voters, husbands, wives and parents and have a commitment to general education.

Staff, too, inherit a school tradition; they are not lecturers or instructors, but teachers. All colleges appoint staff not simply as subject specialists, but as personal and group tutors, responsible for the all-round development of students. All staff are expected to contribute to the total educational task of the college. They are in some sense 'exemplary persons', communicating themselves as well as their subjects.

A sixth form college aims to be a community, though the relatively short stay of students makes this an ideal hard to realize fully. Some stress historical continuity. Ludlow S.F. College traces its history back to the late twelfth century and 'is thus both one of the newest and one of the dozen oldest educational establishments in England'. The college, controlled by the Palmers Company, moved in 1527 into the Palmers Hall building, still in use by the sixth form college, a continuity symbolized by the college crest.

Some colleges have old student associations and in a few, parents' associations have survived. Others have united the two and formed a college association open to past and present students, parents, staff and governors. Not a great deal of the ceremonial of former years survives. In a few colleges Speech Day has been replaced by a presentation evening in December, when former students return to receive certificates. King Edward VI College, Stourbridge maintains its annual Charter Day service which all students are expected to attend. The sense of community depends, of course, on more than ceremonial. It is exemplified through games fixtures, plays and concerts and through expeditions at home and abroad. The college is often actively involved in the local community, while in its own life it tries to display a broad tolerance towards all races and faiths.

But the colleges are not just schools. Whatever the regulations under which they operate and the contacts with secondary education which they cultivate, an institution concerned solely with the post-16 age group and with some students who are legally adult, must differ in important respects from a school. The aims and ethos outlined above cannot be enforced, only commended and exemplified. Finally, therefore, there will be a commitment to personal autonomy and a degree of student self-government. If the college is inspired by liberal principles, then its life must be true to the philosophy it teaches.

Buildings

Only a small proportion of sixth form colleges have been purpose-built, and since the austerity of the 1980's seems likely to rival that of the 1940's, it is unlikely that in the foreseeable future there will be more. Purpose-built colleges like Stoke-on-Trent, South East Essex, Solihull, St Austell, Hereford, Barrow-in-Furness, Eccles and Runshaw have enormous advantages, though even here no clear educational rationale informs their accommodation. Most colleges have to operate in school buildings, often those of a former single sex grammar school, converted more or less successfully to its new role. The quality of the conversion is of enormous importance to the initial success of the college. A distinctive educational ethos and a pattern of mature relationships will largely be the result of a deliberate philosophy and appropriate staff attitudes, but it will nonetheless be greatly helped by suitable buildings. Of the converted colleges, Luton is perhaps the most successful though, as a result of successive development plans over fifteen years, it is beginning to approximate to a new college. The DES still makes no special reference to the needs of 16–19 year olds in its regulations for school premises. Its specified area in square metres for pupils who have attained the age of 15, quaintly states in parenthesis 'including pupils who have attained any higher age'.

There are a number of trends in teaching organization and style which need to be reflected in buildings. There is first of all a move away from exclusive dependence on the expository lesson to a fixed group of 12 to 15 students. A level candidates are not undergraduates and there are pitfalls in lecturing, but the opportunity for an occasional lecture-demonstration to all the A level economists or chemists, for example, suggests the need for one or two lecture theatres, capable of accommodating 70 or 80 students. There should also be smaller rooms, where a teaching group in a minority subject or a seminar group of up to eight students can be taught. Where possible, spaces should be flexible. The open plan style of Cricklade College (a purpose-built tertiary college) may not commend itself to all, but it does move the teaching style away from the teacher as virtuoso performer, towards the student as learner. The division of a room with a partition, often not sound proof, used to turn one satisfactory room for thirty 13 year olds into two unsatisfactory rooms for fifteen 17 year olds, should be avoided when possible.

A second major need is for departmental accommodation, preferably suites of adjacent and intercommunicating rooms, providing teaching and study space, accommodation for the departmental libraries, and resources and bases for staff. The right facilities contribute greatly to the creation of a department which is a team and not just a collection of individuals who happen to teach the same subject.

A third priority will be the college library. However important departmental libraries may be and however far the college's emphasis may move towards resources for learning other than books, no sixth form college should be without an attractively provided, well stocked library staffed by a professional librarian. It should be a place for quiet study, but its role as a library should never be inhibited by restricting access or forbidding movement. Provision for private study is probably best diversified. Most students seem to prefer study carrels in blocks of 20 or so scattered round the college, to study rooms with serried ranks of desks. Increasingly, colleges are emphasizing individual learning, requiring resource areas which make available slide-tape sequences, computers and word processors, geological specimens and mathematical instruments.

Most colleges have a resources centre where reprographic equipment of ever increasing complexity is located, maintained and serviced, together with large items of hardware, such as film projectors and video-recorders. Ideally the resources centre is near to the administration block, with some ancillary staff able to work in both as the work load of each varies during the year. Provision of ancillary staff is rarely adequate and compares unfavourably with the scale of provision in further education. Insufficient account is taken of the burden imposed on office staff by the rapid through-put of students. Laboratories, too, involve heavy use of complex equipment which requires preparation and regular servicing and here again, the provision of ancillary help is rarely adequate.

A good college, like a good school, is concerned with far more than academic work. Since it usually requires full-time attendance and sets out to provide physical recreation, varied cultural activities, leisure pursuits and general education, appropriate facilities must be provided. A sports hall, self-service restaurant, music and drama centre, playing fields and adequate private study areas are all essential. Careers counselling requires a careers suite in continuous use, while offices for senior tutors and interview rooms available for tutors are a necessity.

The student common room is not a haven of civilized social and intellectual life. It is the place where the nature of the sixth form college as a transition from school is most evident, an example of adolescent life-style, individual and collective, with adult restraint removed. The experience of most colleges is that without adult tutelage it becomes a place of deteriorating furniture, mounting piles of litter and even a degree of vandalism. Some colleges find that this is a low price to pay for immunity for the rest of the college from similar depradation. The common room should be large enough to allow a number of students to meet and talk over coffee, and for a variety of activities and of student needs to find expression. Despite the temptation to the contrary it should, as far as the harmonious functioning of the college allows, be left to student control. It is finally one of the distinguishing marks of a sixth form college that, however commodious the common room, groups mark out territory round the building, congregating in small groups on stairs, in corridors or alcoves during private study periods and breaks.

3
Management and staffing

Principal and vice-principals

Secondary schools have headmasters or headmistresses, colleges for the most part have principals. The change of name, however, signifies a difference of style and emphasis more than of job description. The principal is, after all, still the 'headteacher' provided for in the Education Act of 1944 and is legally in loco parentis, though it has not been established whether his duties extend as far as those of the head of a school whose pupils are of compulsory school age. The principal is responsible for the direction of the college, for its overall policy, internal organization, management and discipline, and for the supervision of teaching and non-teaching staff. Public relations is a major commitment. The college relates to a number of contributory schools, to other providers of 16-19 education, to local employers and to the careers service, to universities and to other agencies of higher education, and in each relationship the principal has some part to play—all this in addition to the normal contacts with LEA, governors, parents, the press and outside bodies. In a large college, the principal is likely to know only a sample of students. He may interview those leaving before the end of their course and discuss their plans with one year students who are intending to stay for a further course. He may share in interviewing new entrants and is likely to have a regular meeting with the chairman and committee of the student council. Although he may contribute to the general studies programme or a learning skills course, he is unlikely to find time to undertake a substantial teaching commitment.

His most important role, however, relates to staff. There is no more crucial task than that of appointing staff, within the guidelines laid down by the local authority and in consultation with governors and senior staff. The principal is likely to chair a small policy committee of vice-principals and senior teachers, whose tasks include keeping under review the college's curriculum and pastoral organization, and considering reports from head of department and tutorial committees.

Most colleges have two or three vice-principals, sometimes designated hierarchically as vice-principal, assistant principal and deputy principal, more often differentiated functionally. The usual division is administration, pastoral care and curriculum though the overall arrangement will be such as to ensure interlocking responsibilities and close collaboration. Sometimes responsibility for curriculum is divided between two vice-principals, one concerned with the current curriculum and the making and operation of the timetable, the other with curriculum development, course planning and liaison with heads of departments. The pastoral vice-principal will oversee the tutorial system and student welfare. To this may be added staff development and in-service training, the induction of newcomers to the staff, training of tutors and overseeing probationers. The administrative vice-principal's job is the hardest to define. It involves day to day organization, staff and student bulletin, examinations, resources and finance, health and safety, and responsibility for administrative and laboratory staff. Senior teachers, where such posts are established, are likely to be faculty heads or to be responsible for some major area such as admissions, careers education or the co-ordination of one year courses.

The vertical organization is not, however, universal. Itchen College, Southampton and New College, Telford, have developed a horizontal structure with a vice-principal responsible for new arrivals, induction and the first year in the college, underpinned at Itchen by a senior teacher for one year courses. A second vice-principal takes students through the second and subsequent years of their courses and has responsibility for leavers and links with higher education, while a third vice-principal is concerned with counselling, careers and personnel.

Faculties or departments

About two thirds of all colleges employ the subject department structure usual in schools. The reasons are obvious; it maintains the subject categories in which teachers are trained, it gives an area of known responsibility and is the arrangement traditionally encouraged by the Burnham scale. There are, however, disadvantages. In a small college it leads to a multiplicity of small departments and in a large college to gross disparities between mathematics and English departments which may contain as many as fifteen teachers, and departments such as music or religious studies with one specialist apiece. There may be little cross fertilization of ideas and a tendency to think of the curriculum within rigid subject divisions, while unwieldy meetings of all heads of departments are unlikely to be a fertile source of curriculum innovation.

Some colleges adopt a faculty structure, with subjects grouped in three to seven major areas. This is easily achieved in science and mathematics and in the social sciences where disciplines are related. Outside these, there are problems. The heads of English, history, languages, and religious studies may not be convinced that their interests are represented adequately by a head of humanities faculty whose discipline happens to be geography. A creative arts faculty which includes art, music, home economics, and craft, design and technology may appear to be a marriage of convenience rather than a coherent faculty. What is more, the Burnham scale does not encourage a faculty structure. Though there may be senior teacher posts available to reward the heads of the largest faculties, some will certainly be on the same scale as heads of departments.

A possible solution is a faculty arrangement with a chairman appointed for two or three years with a brief to encourage curriculum development across subject boundaries, to provide a faculty input to the college's general education programme, and to promote joint use of resources.

Three examples of faculty structures

Alton College	Group X 550 students
Arts	English, Languages, Drama, Music, Religious Studies
Creative Design	Art, Design, Domestic Sciences
Science	Sciences, Mathematics, Computing
Social Science	History, Geography, Economics, Sociology, Psychology, Business Studies
Eccles College	Group XI 550 students
Language and Literature	English, Classics, Modern Languages
Social Sciences	Geography, Geology, Economics, Sociology, History
Science	Biology, Chemistry, Physics, Mathematics
Creative Arts	Art and Craft, Music, Drama, P.E.
Stoke-on-Trent S.F. College	Group XIII 1180 students
English Studies	English, Drama
Language Studies	French, Spanish, German, Russian, Latin, Classical, Civilization
Social Studies	Geography, Geology, History, Politics, Economics, Secretarial Studies
Mathematical Studies	Mathematics, Computer Studies
Science Studies	Biology, Chemistry, Physics, Electronics, Engineering Science
General Studies	Art, Home Economics, Technical Studies, Music, Religious Studies, Physical Education, General Studies

Source: *Compendium of Sixth Form and Tertiary Colleges, 1982*

Pastoral organization

The senior tutor, occasionally called division tutor and at Eccles College support tutor, is the key figure in the pastoral organization of the majority of colleges and is in addition normally link tutor to one or more of the college's contributory schools. The number of tutor groups and students placed with each senior tutor varies greatly. At John Leggott College there are ten senior tutors for 750 students, though these include the three vice-principals. At Godalming College senior tutors are each responsible for 220 students, while at Barton Peveril College, Eastleigh, each senior tutor has 130 students, drawn mainly from two of the college's contributory schools. The college is unusual in linking senior tutors directly with students, but not with tutor groups.

The senior tutor system, however, is not without its disadvantages. The existence of a senior tutor may detract from the responsibility of the group tutor. The enthusiastic tutor may find his knowledge of and interest in a student frustrated at a critical stage in the development of their relationship by the student being referred upwards to the senior tutor. Equally, an unenthusiastic tutor may find an excuse for his inadequacy in the knowledge that his omissions will be repaired by the senior tutor. Moreover, the senior tutor can become an administrative and disciplinary official. To be sent to one's senior tutor for permission to take a driving test or to be admonished for truancy or academic fecklessness, may seem to the student all too reminiscent of the school discipline he thought he had grown out of, and to the tutor as detracting from his responsibility for the student's total development.

The strength of the senior tutor system is its simplicity. The division of responsibility between academic and pastoral aspects of college life may create a dichotomy where one does not exist, but it does at least ensure that each receives due emphasis. Staff are closely involved in both, as set tutors on the academic side and as group tutors on the pastoral and administrative side. Through a tutorial committee of senior tutors with the appropriate vice-principal, it provides a means of co-ordinating such things as records and references, the monitoring of student progress, induction fortnight and the use of tutorial time. If most colleges have adopted the senior tutor system, it is because they have found it the most practical way of dealing with a wide variety of pastoral, academic and administrative needs.

About a quarter of all colleges, however, do not base their pastoral organization on the senior tutor. In some colleges overall responsibility rests with the tutorial vice-principal, in others it is shared between three vice-principals. South East Essex S.F. College gives full responsibility to group tutors with reference only to the tutorial vice-principal, and a number of other colleges follow this model.

At some colleges pastoral and academic responsibilities are integrated.

At Skelmersdale College, where half the students are taking a one year course, each of three heads of department is responsible for the academic progress and pastoral care of about 150 students. Each tutor teaches his own tutorial group for at least ten hours a week. At Stoke-on-Trent S.F. College, a very large college with a strong orientation to Advanced level courses, students are placed in one of the College's six major departments. The head of the department allocates them to a tutor group according to their dominant academic interest, and the department thus remains responsible for academic progress and personal development.

A few colleges have preserved pre-reorganization house systems. High Pavement S.F. College, Nottingham, organizes its tutor groups within eight houses, which are also used for competitive sport and drama. King James's College of Henley attaches its tutor groups to three houses in which housemasters oversee student discipline and welfare and house tutors deal with student references and curriculum problems.

The group tutor

If senior tutors are not universal, group tutors certainly are. The number in their group varies from 12 to 20 depending on the authority's staffing and whether new staff are expected to be tutors. The composition of the tutor group varies. The most usual arrangement is a tutor group of both sexes, a variety of courses and subjects and a mixture of contributory schools. This enables senior students to show the ropes to the recruits, introduce them to the student common room and invite them to join the theatre club as well as offering advice about work experience and the ski trip. The dynamics of a tutor group, however, are rarely as predictable or constructive as this. Second year students may instead remain in a superior huddle, while the tutor feels as inhibited by their presence from introducing the college facilities during the tutorial period, as he is from dealing with their UCCA problems.

New College, Telford, and Itchen College, Southampton, organize tutor groups consisting entirely of new students, on the grounds that the needs of a 16 year old entrant are very different from those of a 17 or 18 year old who has been in the college for one or two years. The disadvantage of this arrangement is that the group will have to be proportionately larger in the first year, when individual attention is most needed, and proportionately smaller in the second year when the college is familiar and guidance less needed. Most colleges prefer mixed tutor groups but it is desirable to find means of enabling tutors, particularly in the first half of the autumn term, to have some periods which can be devoted wholly to new students, while the second year have a careers period, a visiting lecturer, or an assembly designed for them.

It may appear to contradict the principle behind an open access college to have separate tutor groups for students on one year courses, and few colleges have done so. In some ways, however, their needs are different. They require careful counselling about the course they should follow and the subjects they should choose. They need careers information at an early stage and specific advice on how to use private study. Left to their own devices, they are more likely than the two year students, to sink rather than swim. They may feel inhibited from asking advice in the presence of students who are abler, more ambitious and more articulate. Separate tutor groups are probably not the right answer, but a tutor for one year courses with a responsibility across the academic/tutorial divide helps to ensure that the specific needs of the one year student are adequately met.

Some colleges, Richard Taunton College, Southampton, among them, organize their tutor groups so that students' interests are 'loosely compatible with the specialization of their tutor, who ideally would teach them. This facilitates getting to know students quickly in a natural setting and creates an immediate bond of common interest. There are, however, disadvantages. An unbalanced group may result; a mathematician may achieve a balanced group but a tutor whose subject is music, home economics or Latin is less likely to do so and this has a knock-on effect elsewhere in the college. What is more, a student whose tutor teaches him for what he comes to regard as other than his main subject, may feel that he has a biased view of his ability and endeavour. There is much to be said for tutor groups composed of a mixture of students, none of whom are taught for their main subject by their tutor. The tutor then devises means of getting to know them all at the beginning of the year and develops a relationship which is quite different from, but complementary to, the teaching relationship.

The work of the group tutor begins with the minimum requirement of registration. Some colleges have dispensed with a formal afternoon registration, some have moved the morning one to break or midday, while many colleges supplement with set registers and a system of reporting late at the office in the morning. For about half the colleges, registration is the only allocated tutor time. Fifteen or twenty minutes is, however, an unsatisfactory period. It is neither brief enough to justify use solely for registration and communication, nor long enough to implement a prepared programme. Colleges solve this problem in a variety of ways. Some expect tutors to arrange individual student interviews at half termly intervals. John Leggott College provides for an hour's tutor period about six times a year when assessments, reports or examination entries are imminent. The core studies at New College, Telford, is based on tutor groups and the tutor sees his students for two or three hours each week, while at St Brendan's (R.C.) College, Bristol, each group tutor takes his own group for religious instruction for the first six weeks of the course. Many colleges, however, allocate a period each week to a tutor session.

The responsibility of the group tutor is to guide students during their stay in the college and to prepare them for their future. At the heart of the task is academic guidance, ensuring that students are on the right course, monitoring their progress through it and ensuring that they have access to careers guidance. Academic development is, however, inseparable from personal development and the tutor group is one means of helping students towards social and emotional maturity, towards an understanding of themselves and other people and towards self-discipline and informed decision making. Tutor groups may operate in a variety of ways, sometimes functioning as a unit, sometimes providing a framework for the discussion of sectional concerns, such as job applications. On other occasions they may offer an opportunity for individual interviews, while other members enjoy a relaxed chat. Senior tutors may build up resources, perhaps including video-tapes or slide sets on personal relationships, study skills or careers development, for optional use by their tutors during the year.

Some colleges use tutorial periods on occasion for a section assembly, for a visiting speaker or a recital by the college choir or orchestra. The tutor group is the place where subject assessments are co-ordinated each half term when the tutor reviews the student's progress. Many colleges include a meeting early in the college year when group tutors can meet parents of new students and establish their responsibility for the student's general welfare. Finally, the tutor group is the unit for elections to the student council and the group's representative reports back after each meeting.

All colleges officially regard the group tutor as central to the work of the college; not all staff see it the same way. Some regard their teaching commitment as a higher priority and prefer the further education title of lecturer. Others find the role expected of the tutor intimidating. For young staff in particular, the work of the group tutor is very demanding. Some are only a few years older than the students in their care; some may lack the emotional detachment necessary to approach what may be highly complex personal issues. There must, therefore, be strong support from senior tutor or vice-principal. Training in tutoring, too, has an invaluable contribution to make. At South East Essex S.F. College all new members of staff, at whatever level they enter the college, serve a year's apprenticeship with an experienced tutor and thereafter all are available for tutoring. During the summer examination period, there is a two day briefing for all who will become tutors the following September, with sessions led by tutors whose experience ranges from one year upwards. Some sessions are devoted to a full examination of the college's administrative practices. More important, however, is the discussion of case histories, to provide experience of advising in a variety of situations, and also workshop sessions of student interviews. Hampshire organizes a two-day course at the end of the summer term at its residential centre in the New Forest, to which tutors from the county's twelve colleges come. They are joined for one day by a selection of students who contribute their angle on the work of the tutor.

Deployment of staff

Sixth form colleges fall into Burnham groups VIII to XIV. Only Luton and Loreto S.F.C., Manchester, are in Group XIV, though several more would have been, had not the Houghton Report reduced the points allowance for pupils of 16 and above.

Group	VIII	IX	X	XI	XII	XIII	XIV
Number of colleges	1	10	17	40	18	14	2

Source: *Compendium of Sixth Form and Tertiary Colleges 1982*

These bald facts, however, conceal complex problems associated with the deployment of staff in a college. There is first of all, a substantial disparity in the staffing allowed by different authorities for the age group. No consensus exists nationally about the ratio of staff to students needed to enable the college adequately to make its contribution to the 'spiritual, moral, mental and physical development of the community', as is required by the Education Act of 1944. The ratio in some authorities is 1:9, in others 1:14, with a tendency for ratios to worsen in recent years. In 1975 the average was 1:9.2; by January 1980 it was 1:10.6.

The allocation of staff is usually calculated by taking the average participation rate for the area over the previous three or four years and applying that to the number expected to leave the comprehensive schools in the current year. Many authorities base their estimate on the Form 7 figure for the following January. There is normally a drop-out of perhaps 5% of the September entry by January, a factor which is inevitable and even desirable if students are to be given the opportunity to sample the college and conclude that it is not for them. Colleges are, however, rarely staffed to allow for the additional students in the first term of the year or for the seventh term Oxford and Cambridge candidates who leave in December.

What, then, is the staff/student ratio required to provide for a college? There are three variables in the calculation.

1 Teacher contact time (TCT)
This is the proportion of the college working week during which staff will be timetabled with a class, whether for examination work, general

studies, recreational activities, or tutorial time. Non-contact time means time allocated for preparation, marking and informal contact with students, all in themselves a heavier commitment in a sixth form college than in an 11-18 school. If the college week contains notionally 25 hours, then 0.8 teacher contact will mean that staff overall teach 20 hours. To make allowance for the pastoral, administrative and liaison work of vice-principals, senior tutors, heads of departments and careers staff, the contact hours of the remaining staff will need to be about 22 hours. If a college's notional week contains 30 hours, then a contact ratio of about 0.66 will be assumed.

2 Student contact ratio (SCR)

This is the proportion of the college working week during which students will be taught by staff, as distinct from undertaking private study. For some students this will be as low as 0.7 of a 25 hour week, for others taking a City and Guilds Foundation course or a secretarial course, as high as 0.9. Colleges usually aim at about 0.8 or about 20 hours contact per week.

3 Set size (SS)

A series of conflicting norms affect set size, both for A level and sub-A level teaching groups.
   a) Highly skilled staff should be deployed with economic groups.
   b) Set sizes should not be over-large; size should not inhibit individual attention to students both in class and in the marking of written work.
   c) Subjects with minority appeal, such as second and third foreign languages, Latin, music and religious studies should be safeguarded.

The first two conditions suggest that A level groups should normally fall into the 8-14 range. Below this there is loss of intellectual stimulus, above this figure teaching techniques may be limited and students receive insufficient individual attention.

The third condition will require on occasion that sets below five will be timetabled. The college will consequently be obliged to provide larger classes for O level and CEE groups. These students are, however, of substantially lower ability than O level candidates in the fifth form and it is inequitable to provide less generously for them than for high ability A level candidates.

The deployment of staff which results from this model can be calculated. We assume for the sake of simplicity, in the example below, a college of 600 students, a working week of 25 hours, a teacher contact ratio of 0.8 and a student contact ratio of 0.8.

Teacher contact hours required (T) = $\dfrac{\text{Students on roll}}{\text{Average set size}} \times$ Student contact ratio $\times$ Hours in the working week

$$T = \dfrac{600}{12} \times 0.8 \times 25$$
$$= 1000$$

Total staff required (S) = $\dfrac{\text{Teacher contact hours}}{\text{Teacher contact ratio} \times \text{Total hours in working week}}$

$$S = \dfrac{1000}{0.8} \times 25$$
$$= 50$$

Staff/student ratio (R) = $\dfrac{\text{Total number of students}}{\text{Total number of staff}}$

$$R = \dfrac{600}{50}$$
$$= 1:12$$

It follows that if the staffing ratio is less generous than 1:12, then either staff must teach longer hours, students receive less class contact, or set sizes rise. As we have seen, sixth form colleges have, for the most part, been staffed more generously than 1:12. Many principals would argue that a ratio of 1:12 is the point beyond which the quality of what the college offers suffers unacceptably. In particular its commitment to general education cannot be fulfilled.

Staff experience of the college

To many teachers, sixth form colleges are an unknown territory. Under 6,000 out of a secondary teaching profession of 231,000 or 2.6%, are currently employed in them. Nor have sixth form colleges yet had time to produce from their students more than a small proportion of those entering the teaching profession. Few post-graduate certificate courses pay much attention to preparation for teaching the 16–19 age group, or arrange visits to sixth form colleges. Teaching practice shared between an 11–16 school and a college is sometimes attempted, but it is rarely wholly satisfactory. In a recent survey of 187 staff in their first posts in 51 colleges, 8% had been pupils in a college and 10% had spent part of their teaching practice in one, while 54% had no previous experience of a sixth form college.

Once in the college, however, many staff come to see their future in 16–19 education. Over 70% of those who took part in the survey intended their next post to be teaching the 16–19 age group, 53% in a sixth form college, 18% in further education. Some are highly qualified mathematics and science graduates who would not, but for the college, have entered teaching at all, while others would have taught in a large grammar or independent school where a high proportion of sixth form work is available.

Promotion prospects in sixth form colleges are limited. Relatively few senior posts fall vacant and competition is fierce. The college needs its own staff development and in-service programme. This might include periodic changes of role within the college, the opportunity to contribute to staff working parties and to gain experience by visits to other colleges. Some colleges operate a junior staff committee which is a means of involving them in discussions on college policy and plans. About half the senior appointments made in recent years from outside the colleges have been made from comprehensive schools, reflecting the value of comprehensive experience in the open access college. Although staff move to appointments in further education or tertiary colleges, movement in the opposite direction is limited. The different salary scale, the requirement of teacher training and probation for qualified teacher status in a sixth form college, and the further education Conditions of Service agreement all constitute barriers.

Staff find contact with older students, the adult atmosphere and academically demanding work, rewarding aspects of teaching in the college. Many enjoy work as a group tutor, being able to get to know students on a variety of courses, with different backgrounds and needs, and to guide them through this crucial period of their lives. Others comment upon the sense of purpose which arises in part from the brevity of the course. Pleasure, however, is not entirely unalloyed. Sixth form colleges impose a heavy administrative burden on all staff, arising from admission and leaving procedures and the need to prepare a plethora of reports and references. The examination orientation of much of the work places great responsibility on all staff, and this weighs heavily on the young and inexperienced. Probationers carry a burden of examination work which would not arise in a school, whether grammar or comprehensive. The load of preparation and marking is considerable and staff accept a great deal of evening work as an essential part of the job. There is some compensation in the months of June and July, when the external examinations bring the opportunity to undertake much needed preparation. Excessive examination work can have a deadening effect and it is essential to introduce variety if the diet of staff in a sixth form college is not to become indigestible. Many staff welcome the opportunity to contribute to the college's recreational programme and to offer courses which are unconstrained and unorthodox, to introduce new and experimental syllabuses, and to teach at a variety of levels.

4

Curriculum and examinations

Curriculum constraints: GCE A and O level

Since 1960 there have been substantial changes in the curriculum of secondary schools resulting from comprehensive reorganization and the catalytic effect of the Schools Council and other bodies. Further changes will follow if O level and CSE are replaced by a common examination at 16 plus. In Further Education, too, there has been substantial curriculum change. The needs of industry and commerce have led to restructuring of courses and the emergence of new ones through the Business Education Council and the Technician Education Council. More recently, the Further Education Curriculum Review and Development Unit (FE-CRDU) set up by the DES in 1977, has produced a series of reports of which *A Basis for Choice* is likely to have widespread and influential effects far beyond FE (**16**). The sixth form curriculum by contrast has remained remarkably static. Here external constraints have inhibited, rather than encouraged, change. The universities, though a minority user of A level, have ensured that the examination structure remains unchanged. If A level were to be replaced by a less specialized examination, they have argued, it would be necessary either to extend the first degree course to four years, or to acquiesce in a significant reduction in academic standards, neither of which could be contemplated. Taken with the conservatism of the teaching profession and the lack of a central body able to enforce, as distinct from recommend, change, this has effectively frustrated proposals for reforming the sixth form curriculum.

The fundamental criticism of the curriculum is that it is overspecialized and unduly concerned with subject content as distinct from conceptual knowledge and interdisciplinary skills. 'When a pupil enters the sixth form,' wrote Crowther in 1959, 'he becomes a specialist, that is to say the subjects of his serious intellectual study are confined to two or three.' Crowther was not unduly concerned by this situation, though the report drew attention publicly for the first time to the need for some compensatory balance to be introduced into the curriculum of those who, at 16, had already embarked on the specialist study of either science or arts subjects.

The succeeding years have seen three parallel movements concerned with the reform of the sixth form curriculum. The first followed Crowther's suggestions and led to the appearance of General Studies in the curriculum. The second reform movement took place within subject syllabuses themselves. Examination syllabuses and methods of examining at Advanced level influence to a remarkable extent both the content of the course and the methods of teaching throughout the two years in the sixth form. If we wish, therefore, to change teaching styles, we must change syllabuses and examining methods. There has been steady but substantial piecemeal reform of both. Nuffield Science is intended to initiate students into scientific methods, to encourage conjecture, experiment and refutation, to introduce an open-ended approach and to change the style of both learning and teaching. Few subjects have been untouched by such changes. Modern syllabuses are prefaced by statements of aims and objectives. Sociology and economics, amongst others, include questions requiring response to quantitative data, whilst multiple choice tests, once confined to lower level examinations, have been refined for use at A level. Course work and individual projects are included in the assessment of subjects such as geography and biology.

It is the third strand of reform on which most effort has been expended and to least effect. The three subject curriculum continues to dominate the scene in the 1980's as it did in the 1950's. The pioneering efforts of A.D.C. Peterson, head of the Oxford University Department of Educational Studies in the early 1960's, were taken over by the Schools Council and resulted in a series of proposals for radical change. The final one, for a five subject curriculum at two levels, Normal and Further, was launched in *Working Paper 47* in 1973 and worked out in detail in non-operational studies, under the aegis of syllabus steering groups for each academic subject. The rejection of the N and F proposals in 1979 leaves the sixth form with a curriculum structure which was designed in the immediate post-war years for a very much smaller and more homogeneous sixth form population. It is hard to believe that A level is adequate as the staple diet for the sixth form of the last two decades of the century. It is, however, even harder to conceive a process which might dethrone it.

The sixth form curriculum is what Basil Bernstein calls a 'collection curriculum'. The student's course has no set of aims but consists of a number of discrete subjects. Colleges face the dilemma that if a student loses interest in a subject, finds it difficult or obtains an offer of a place in an institution of higher education requiring qualifications in only two subjects, it will be hard to insist on continued attendance at the third. Second, we are left with a curriculum dominated by external examinations. When the examination arrives, the course ends. For all the theory that curriculum precedes examinations, the reverse is in practice truer. Third, specialization continues. There has been a steady move away from the dominance of course choices consisting entirely of arts or of science subjects. The growth of social sciences has helped to bridge the gap while mathematics frequently forms part of all types of course. Scientists, however, still tend to choose three subjects from mathematics, physics, chemistry and biology, though computer science and electronic systems are also found increasingly. It is the weaker scientist, who most needs the reinforcement of studying two related A levels, who is likely to replace one or more with economics or psychology. A three subject curriculum is simply not flexible enough to provide a means of avoiding undue specialization.

It is perhaps surprising that more use has not been made of the International Baccalaureate, an examination pioneered in this country at Atlantic College and now used at over 150 schools worldwide. It provides an examined course in six subjects chosen from five areas: mother tongue, a foreign language, mathematics, science and the study of man. Three are offered at higher level and three at subsidiary level, while all students in addition take part in social, creative or aesthetic activities for half a day each week and follow a course in the theory of knowledge intended to provide perspectives to the whole course. The diploma awarded following satisfactory performance is accepted by all universities in Britain and by most overseas(**25, 26**). It probably appears too ambitious and too demanding for the average A level student, its language requirement enough to daunt most. Its image is of the high flier who is specially selected for Atlantic College. It appears to presuppose a boarding school and a staff commitment well beyond the normal. The break with excessive specialization without the sacrifice of depth, the integration of general and examination studies and the theory of knowledge paper merit further consideration. A number of sixth form colleges expressed interest in a pilot scheme in 1979, but the necessary funding from the Schools Council was not then available.

A second development which has proved successful in recent years is the modular curriculum, pioneered in British higher education by the Open University and in further education by the City and Guilds and the Business and Technician Education Councils. Maurice Holt in his book *The Tertiary Sector* suggests as a means of integrating the sixth form curriculum an Advanced National Diploma on modular lines, 'Advanced' showing its equivalence with GCE Advanced level and 'National', the level of TEC and BEC course with which it would correspond(**24**).

The reconstruction of the sixth form curriculum is an urgent need. Perhaps sixth form colleges, with their larger numbers and their commitment in this area, might provide a vehicle and succeed where others have failed. Meanwhile, each college is left to construct its own curriculum with the building blocks provided by examination syllabuses only partly designed for the purpose.

Advanced level

The basis of the academic work of all sixth form colleges is GCE Advanced level. The average number of subjects offered by colleges is 27, though the range varies from 45 at Itchen College, Southampton and 36 at Queen Mary's College, Basingstoke to 18 or 19, offered by some of the smaller colleges and those which prefer to retain the traditional academic choice. The larger colleges, those with over 700 students, are likely to offer 30 or more. Wide choice combined with economical provision is part of the justification of a break at 16. But how wide? The Macfarlane Report pointed out that while 12-16 subjects would be a reasonable choice in a single institution, this would place in jeopardy all modern languages except French and German, classical languages and ancient history, religious studies, geology, politics and law as well as home economics, technical subjects, engineering science and electronics. It concluded that 25 subjects should be available in each area though not necessarily in one institution.

There are, however, issues to be faced, even in the larger colleges. The predominance of the major subjects is overwhelming, however wide the choice offered. Even in large colleges minority subjects may recruit groups which are only marginally economic or where viability will not be established until September. Some new subjects attract students whose choice is determined by dissatisfaction with subjects previously studied or by the glamour of a subject of whose real nature they have no knowledge. The decision to offer a wide choice of subjects needs, then, the support of staff, since it is likely to place an extra burden on those who teach well-subscribed subjects. A wide choice of syllabuses within a subject is also likely to result in uneven group sizes. The wider the choice of subjects and syllabuses offered to students, the greater the preparatory information needed and the skill and care required in counselling, both before students arrive and during their early weeks in the college.

Languages are strongly represented in sixth form colleges, with some offering as many as six or seven modern and classical languages. Eleven colleges offer Italian and 23 Russian. Numbers in languages other than French and German rarely exceed single figures in any one year at A level. The sex imbalance continues to cause concern, with girls as dominant in modern languages and English as are the boys in physics and further mathematics. Seventeen colleges offer a full classics course of Greek, Latin and ancient history while a further six offer Latin and Greek, and 34 colleges the recently introduced classical civilization. Stoke-on-Trent S.F. College offers a three year course in Russian and German to those who have not previously studied the language. Numbers have remained small but the opportunity is there for a committed linguist.

Many colleges offer a variety of syllabuses within a subject. Some are

Availability of Advanced level subjects in Sixth Form Colleges, 1981-1982

All colleges	80-99		60-79	
Art	Music	89	Latin	73
Biology	Religious Studies	87	Geology	69
Chemistry	Home Economics	86	Political Studies	68
Economics			Spanish	67
English Literature			Sociology	66
French			Computer Studies	64
Further Mathematics				
Geography				
German				
History				
Mathematics				
Physics				

40-59		20-39		10-19	
General Studies	47	Design		Engineering	
Technical Drawing	38	Technology	38	Science	19
		Classical		History of Art	19
		Civilization	35	Electronic	
		Business Studies	32	Systems	17
		Social Biology	32	Metalwork	15
		Geometrical and		Statistics	15
		Engineering		Human Biology	14
		Drawing	27	Woodwork	14
		Design	26	Environmental	
		Greek	24	Studies	12
		Ancient History	23	Italian	11
		Russian	23	Psychology	11
		Theatre Arts	22		
		Economic History	20		

Subjects listed by fewer than 10 colleges include: Botany, Communication Studies, Economics and World Affairs, Economic Geography, English Language and Literature, French Language and Society, Home Family and Society, Industrial Studies, Photography, Physical Science, Welsh, Zoology.

Source: Compendium of Sixth Form and Tertiary Colleges, 1982

to meet *different academic needs:* pure mathematics with statistics for biologists, economists and geographers, pure and applied mathematics for physicists and engineers, and further mathematics for those who intend to read mathematics at university. No college offers fewer than three mathematics syllabuses and some as many as seven or eight together with accountancy or statistics as separate subjects. Some offer both traditional and Nuffield syllabuses to meet the needs of different contributory schools or the preferences or abilities of students. Biology appears as human biology and social biology as well as biology both traditional and Nuffield. Varied art syllabuses are frequently available including ceramics, graphics, photography, art history, sculpture and fabric printing as well as drawing and painting. Many students have the opportunity of choosing between medieval, renaissance and modern history and of deciding whether to offer a project alongside the written papers. Solihull holds the record with seven history syllabuses.

Sixth form colleges offer an opportunity to experiment with new A level syllabuses, for example: communication studies, English language and literature, French with a language emphasis, environmental studies, electronic systems, theatre arts, law, and psychology.

Practical subjects have sometimes presented difficulties. A former boys' school is not usually equipped to offer home economics at A level. About 15 colleges do not teach it through lack of facilities, though some have an arrangement with the local technical college. Without provision of A level courses, however, sub-A level courses will not be available nor will the essential contribution to the general studies programme. The same applies to technical subjects in the former girls' schools.

Ordinary level

Ordinary level represents the second major examination taken in sixth form colleges but is even less satisfactory than A level. In their work on one year courses, Dennis Vincent and Judy Dean scrutinized O level results. 365 students who were candidates for O level after their sixth year in school already held an average of 1.3 pass grades when they embarked on the course. They took 4.2 subjects and passed at the end of the year in 1.4. This meagre result is often disguised by failing to distinguish the various categories of O level student in the sixth form. An overall pass rate of 50% may conceal the poor results of those whose staple programme it has provided**(46)**.

O level is used for a variety of purposes:

By students taking A level
An O level subject selected from a wide range, may be used to support two A levels, either because the student is unable to sustain three A levels, or because he prefers to take only two A levels and an ancillary O level

is needed to produce an acceptable timetable. Two different O level subjects may then be taken in consecutive years. Few colleges now offer two year O level courses and if they do it is only in a narrow range of subjects. A second category may be a student using O level as a means of consolidating basic knowledge on the way to A level in subjects not previously studied such as economics or geology. A third group will be those trying to overcome earlier failure in a subject essential for qualification, usually English language, mathematics or a foreign language.

By students who have failed O level
A substantial number of students will be retrieving previous failure, taking between four and six subjects, with English language and mathematics as compulsory unless success has already been achieved. College policy varies. Some favour a restricted course of four subjects, providing the same class contact time as for an A level subject, probably four to five hours. Other colleges expect students to take five or six subjects, with less contact time. Others have two categories of O level, half box and full box (see page **64**) depending on the subject and the likely student take-up. There is a dilemma whether the student should undertake new subjects (the benefit of freshness offset by the short time to master new content and perhaps teaching methods), or to retake old ones (with the danger of boredom after two years already spent on the same syllabus). The usual advice is a mixture, the freshness of the new off-setting the boredom of the familiar.

By students converting from CSE
Many students come to the college with the expectation that the debased currency of CSE can be freshly minted into O level currency which has retained its value. O level is, however, an examination designed for the top quarter of the ability range and only a small proportion can expect that an extra year will enable them to reach the standard which it demands. In many subjects the style of work required is wholly different from CSE, more disciplined and less imaginative, dependent on a grasp of concise English, factual recall and the ability to write essays—skills which the candidate lacked at 15 and may not be able to acquire in nine months. The problem is compounded if the various categories are taught together. This may be a matter of necessity or principle but the teaching problems are formidable.

Curriculum considerations: other courses

Though GCE A and O level form the bulk of the sixth form college curriculum, they do not constitute the whole of it, and it is around the remainder that the most important debate is taking place. There has in the past been a broad distinction between the approach to the curriculum taken by schools and by further education. The school curriculum has been liberal, academic, subject based, concerned with the upper levels of ability and with providing a preparation for entry to higher education. The FE curriculum has been utilitarian, technical, vocational and course based. It has been designed for those of average ability, and its students have subsequently entered working life or gone on to other courses in further education. The distinction has, however, in recent years become blurred. Schools have widened their horizons, introduced link courses and work experience, widened subject syllabuses and recognized that by no means all sixth formers are qualified for or interested in entry to higher education. At the same time an increasing number of students have entered FE colleges, to take A levels with the intention of entering universities and polytechnics. Within FE there has been an increasing emphasis on games, general studies and pastoral care. The traditional distinction, exemplified by the contrast between education and training, has been breaking down.

It seems likely that the government will now take a hand in nudging schools further in the direction of the changes which have already begun to happen. *Examinations 16–18*, a consultative paper, was published by the DES and the Welsh Office in October 1980. It was concerned in particular with the examination structure for 'young people of broadly average ability with modest examination achievements at 16-plus who intend to enter employment at 17-plus and who do not wish to take or resit school based examinations'. There must, it argued, be a single structure, whether such young people chose to remain at school or to enter a sixth form or further education college, and a major purpose must be 'assisting the transition from school to work'. A new examination, therefore, must be vocationally oriented. Over a year earlier the FECRDU had produced *A Basis for Choice* (often called the Mansell Report after the then Chairman of FECRDU, Mr Jack Mansell). It was this report, concerned with the needs of further education, which provided the consultative paper with the model for its new examination proposals. At the same time, it rejected the school based CEE which had been the subject of the Keohane Report, also published in 1979. *A Basis for Choice* did not present an examination structure but rather 'a set of criteria which present and future schemes might satisfy'. The basic course occupying a minimum of 730 out of the 1000 hours available, would comprise core studies (60%), vocational studies (20%) and job specific studies (20%). For the core studies an ambitious list of twelve aims was suggested and each was worked out in a series of objectives. It was further proposed that the course should be assessed, not only by examinations, but by means of a comprehensive profile. Shortly after the appearance of *Examinations 16–18* the Macfarlane Report *Education for 16–19 Year Olds* appeared. This came to a similar conclusion, arguing that for the target group a Mansell model was appropriate. 'We look for the development of courses with a strong pre-employment character. We think it is of the greatest importance that employers should come to value such a form of post-16 education as a preparation for employment, and be ready to accord it due recognition alongside the more traditional A level, O level and CSE courses.' (paragraph 39)

The refusal to validate CEE, together with the publication of these papers, gives an indication of the future direction of full-time education for students not taking the traditional GCE and CSE examinations. The emphasis in future will be vocational and practical rather than academic, and course based rather than subject based. There will be a strong emphasis on basic communication skills, literacy and numeracy, and on preparation for working life.

The immediate reaction of schools was defensive, fearing that general education beyond 16 would be lost, that pre-employment courses would be utilitarian, that experience gained in CEE would be wasted and that schools would be ill-equipped to compete with FE in the provision of the new courses. The development of Mansell courses will have to be a joint endeavour between schools and further education. The vocational and practical emphasis need not be seen as an end in itself, but as providing the motivation and integration necessary to a sound general education, which were often missing in subjects and syllabuses conceived more generally. Nor need insights and experience gained in CEE be lost. It is clear that some of the rigidities apparent in the original proposals will be modified when operational Mansell courses are considered further**(17)**.

CEE and CSE

So much for the future. Meanwhile, colleges have proved to be a major user of the CEE and the doubt which hangs over its future does not seem to have reduced its importance in the curriculum, which on the contrary has grown. As the proportion of average and below average ability 16 year olds have entered the colleges, partly as an alternative to unemployment, so courses made up partly of CEE subjects have been offered to them. If the uptake of CEE has not been as high as originally predicted, opponents attribute this to its limited appeal, while supporters point to the failure of successive governments to validate it. It has, as a result, failed to gain recognition from employers, parents and the general public. It is more used by girls than boys and a high proportion of its users take only one or two subjects rather than the full programme of five subjects originally envisaged. It is, however, highly valued by its users, providing in the words of the Keohane Report, 'the spur of a new syllabus and the satisfaction of a sixth form approach'. The majority of sixth form colleges offer CEE though many provide only a few subjects. Luton, Ashford, Itchen and Barnsley are among the colleges which in 1980 offered nearly 20 subjects, while at Stoke, CEE rather than O level is the major component of all one year courses. Its use is chiefly to provide an appropriate level in some subjects for some students, the remainder of whose course consists of O levels, if they are at the higher end of the ability range, and RSA or courses validated by the college, if they are at the lower end. It is also sometimes used as a third subject by students taking two A levels. Many colleges use CEE in mathematics and English rather than O level, because the syllabuses are more varied and the style of examining more appropriate at this age, while the likelihood of obtaining an O level equivalent is strong. In some parts of the country the CEE is not available and colleges use CSE to enable students to obtain qualifications which they failed to achieve in the fifth form.

Had the Keohane Report been accepted the CEE would have been different from its present form. It would have been a free standing examination with its own certificate and it would have been unrelated to either CSE or O level. There were to have been three gradings: pass with merit, pass, and fail; in addition there would have been compulsory proficiency tests in English and mathematics, graded in the same way and available three or four times each year(**22**).

Pre-vocational courses

Some of the students who now enter sixth form colleges are amongst those who have never been highly motivated by traditional school subjects and it is in part to meet their needs that colleges have embarked on new course structures. Some are provided by examining bodies whose main clientele has hitherto been in further education, while others are the result of the college's own curriculum development. Since 1976 the foundation courses of the City and Guilds of London Institute have been available to schools and colleges and by 1980 had been adopted in about 20 sixth form colleges, some using one, others a number. Each foundation course is a one year programme based on a group of related occupations and industries:

art and design	food industries
community care	nursing and allied occupations
commercial studies	public and recreational services
distribution	science industries
engineering	technology

There are six main components with a broad occupational focus within which the college is free to design its course relevant to the needs of its students:

1   industrial and environmental studies
2   skills and practices
3   technology, theory and science

4   communication studies including English (written and oral) and numeracy for everyday life and work
5   guidance education through both group and individual counselling
6   optional activities, such as music, art, pottery, languages, local history, sport and outdoor pursuits

At the end of the course, students receive a certificate giving a detailed profile based on course work and examinations. There is a four point scale—distinction, credit, pass and fail—in each of eight components, all of which must be passed to obtain the certificate.

Itchen College introduced three City and Guilds foundation courses in 1978 offering engineering, distribution and communication studies to a total of 33 students. Those who came had experienced minimum success at school and were lacking in both self confidence and motivation. The college evaluated this first course carefully. Two thirds of the students who began the course completed it and obtained a certificate. Only four, when asked, said they regretted coming to college and lack of money and the demands of homework were the chief reasons. Students on the course had appreciated membership of mixed tutor groups. Some were entered also for subjects at CEE, CSE and RSA. Just as important as the additional qualifications which they obtained was the personal progress made. Staff felt that they were more mature, more socially adjusted and employable, as well as more confident with both staff and fellow students, in groups and individually. These are findings which are endorsed by other colleges which have embarked on courses of this type for their one year students(**43**).

Skelmersdale College bases its community care course on the City and Guilds foundation course, its pre-tec course on either science industries or engineering. The pre-catering course makes use of the food industries foundation course and includes O level and CSE subjects as well as work experience in hotels and restaurants.

The examinations of the Royal Society of Arts have also gained currency in sixth form colleges, particularly as a validation for secretarial courses and about half of the colleges offer shorthand, typewriting, audio-typing and office practice. Many provide two or more secretarial courses. Two year students take two A levels in addition to secretarial subjects and there may be an opportunity to take the Private Secretary's Certificate of the London Chamber of Commerce. The one year continuation course is for those whose school subjects included typewriting, while the beginners course is for those who have done no typewriting before. Both include subjects at O level or CEE. The Royal Society of Arts examinations in English and mathematics are sometimes used to provide a lower level and more vocationally oriented course.

It seems likely that the next few years will see an expansion into schools of the examinations of the recently created Technician Education Council (TEC) and Business Education Council (BEC). Both councils were set up in the early 1970s in the wake of the Haslegrave Report of 1969 on technician level courses. It is BEC General which is relevant to the work of sixth form colleges, though at the moment it is normally only available in collaboration with a further education college. Like the City and Guilds foundation courses there is a compulsory core of study. Option modules are added to meet specific vocational requirements. There are in addition four central themes running through the modules: an understanding of the role of money in business, an understanding of the role of people in business life, the capacity for clear self expression and a familiarity with analytical techniques, and the problems of work in a technological environment. Skelmersdale College and Runshaw College, Leyland are two of the sixth form colleges which have embarked on BEC courses. At Skelmersdale, students take the compulsory modules People and Communication (English), Business Calculations (mathematics), and the World of Work (commerce), and then choose from among option modules which include consumer law, data processing, bookkeeping, typewriting, and telephonist and receptionist skills. The college also offers a TEC certificate course in conjunction with Wigan College of Technology. In the first year students take mathematics, physical science and community studies at the sixth form college and the practical units at Wigan, selecting, for example, motor vehicle maintenance, electronics or science. In the second year they are enrolled full-time at Wigan College of Technology.

A number of colleges have their own schemes of collaboration in pre-vocational courses. Bexhill College runs a pre-nursing course in collaboration with Hastings District School of Nursing with one day a week spent on placement in one of the six local hospitals. General Education takes place at the sixth form college with a valuable vocational slant. The pre-health service course at Skelmersdale College is a two year course suitable for those interested in nursing, radiography, physiotherapy or occupational therapy. This, too, includes a one day placement in a hospital. There are two programmes, one for those who need an A level which is offered in Social Biology, and the other providing O levels in Welfare and Society and Human Biology. The Certificate of Further Education in Pre-Nursing Studies is taken by suitable candidates on both courses. Some colleges' pre-nursing courses make use of the examinations of the National Association of Maternity and Child Welfare.

Another area in which colleges offer pre-vocational courses is physical education, often oriented towards those intending to offer PE in a teacher training course as well as those considering careers in the police, the armed services, physiotherapy, remedial gymnastics or the recreation industry. Bilborough College, Nottingham, offers for the former an opportunity to visit Carnegie and Loughborough colleges, and work experience in local schools as well as courses in the college in the anatomy and physiology of exercise, first aid and a variety of physical activities including hiking, canoeing and camping.

Sixth form colleges have been impelled in the direction indicated by *A Basis for Choice* partly by the desire to meet the needs of their expanding clientele, partly through the realization that pre-vocational courses need not be narrowly conceived and partly by the improvement in motivation which is evident. John Leggott College, Scunthorpe, responded to increasing unemployment and to the growing number of students entering the college with CSE grade 4 and below, by offering a one year general vocational preparation course along the lines suggested by *A Basis for Choice*. In order to give staff experience before devising their own course, use was made of the City and Guilds Foundation Course framework. Alongside the guide scheme in engineering, the college has devised its own course entitled Food, Family and Community. This is at present externally certificated by the City and Guilds but alongside, the college is using the Humberside Profile Assessment and intends to move entirely to profile assessment in its own course in future. Barnsley S.F. College now has three pre-vocational courses, two run in cooperation with the local college of technology. One, in the technology area, will lead to TEC Level 1; a second, in the caring skills, will lead to the Yorkshire and Humberside Certificate of Further Education; a third leads to the City and Guilds Certificate in Food Industries.

New College, Telford, is one of the few colleges operating one of the pilot schemes for *A Basis for Choice*, a course known as General Vocational Preparation run in conjunction with the City and Guilds(**17**). It consists of four elements: arithmetic, English, the world of work and ancillary courses, as well as work experience and participation in the college's core studies and recreational studies programme. The programme is common to the group, except for ancillary courses where students choose between three and five from a list which includes catering, laboratory skills, computing, basic engineering and community care. The world of work section includes New College Enterprises which involves setting up, registering and running a business. Shares are sold, a product or service is selected, wages are paid and rent is incurred for the use of college premises(**42**).

There is already sufficient experience of these courses to indicate that they are practicable within the framework of a sixth form college and that they can retain the best of school based liberal education, as well as awakening the motivation and achieving the vocational relevance which are essential at this age. The impetus provided by government policy will give sixth form colleges the opportunity, and perhaps the resources, to expand their provision further in this area.

Foundation courses

Faced with a steadily rising number of students of below average ability, the response of sixth form colleges has been to develop their own courses, sometimes entirely certificated within the college, sometimes using existing examinations to validate part of the course.

The Foundation Course at South East Essex S.F. College, developed originally in 1972 and modified each year, is aimed at students with an ability range from CSE 4 to ESN(M) and has grown steadily in popularity. Members of the course join the college's normal tutorial groups but their work is organized in a group of 10-12 students drawn from the course's full ability range. The theme of the course is *survival*, with five consecutive work units:

1. *Survival at college*—study skills, information location, problem solving, individual rights and obligations.
2. *Basic survival*—food, clothing, shelter.
3. *Community*—physical, political, economic, social and cultural, beliefs. The third world and relations between the first, second and third worlds.
4. *Relationships*—sex education, family, marriage, gender, race, friendship, spiritual love.
5. *Work*—why work? what does it mean? basic economics, getting a job, unemployment, alternatives.

The method, however, is as important as the message, with an emphasis on experiencing and participating. Students take part in a number of cooperative ventures, for example, running a secondhand book shop, craft-work sales and the organization of a bank to finance them. There are other activities outside the classroom using surveys and questionnaires, and two integrated days during the year when students undertake a series of tasks and problems, the solution of which draws on the skills and knowledge derived from the work units already completed. There is a residential week at Thaxted. More conventional skills may be tested by taking English, mathematics and geography at CEE. The main assessment, however, is by profile under the headings numeracy, communication, life skills and social understanding, together with comments on ability to work with others, effort, staying power and concentration, responsibility and maturity(**19,42**).

The College Certificate Course at Price's College, Fareham, was devised for ESN(M) school leavers. Since the raising of the school leaving age these 16 year olds have lost the extra year which had, until then, in part compensated for lost time earlier. They often mature late and need time to reach the stage of personal development already attained by academically abler pupils, while their learning capacity makes considerable strides at about sixteen, just as compulsory schooling is coming to an end. Their employment prospects are relatively poor and a gentler introduction to adult life is needed than that provided by a period of unemployment. The course offers an internally validated certificate. It caters not only for officially designated ESN(M) students, but also for those of limited ability, often from the remedial departments of the college's contributory schools, as well as referrals from special agencies. It aims to prepare students for the world of work and for living as independent adults in society.

The objectives are organized through five concurrent modules, each colour coded with attractive titles, which can easily be recognized by both staff and students.

1 *Earning a living*—including two periods of work experience.
2 *Setting up home*—finding, furnishing and maintaining a home.
3 *Living with others*—personal, social and political relationships.
4 *Going places*—from vehicle maintenance to booking an air ticket and including a residential visit to London.
5 *Living with leisure*

In order to integrate the course into the life of the college, a deliberate decision was made not to appoint specialist staff, but to involve the large number of existing staff who were interested. This was further achieved by including college certificate students in tutor groups, though for convenience in two only of the college's six senior tutor divisions, and involving them in the games and general studies programme. Some staff took the City and Guilds qualification 'Teaching the Handicapped in Further Education', and the course director, initially a member of the geography department and subsequently a senior tutor, took the Open University course on 'The Handicapped in the Community'.

Much of the material in the five modules is taught using resource based learning in a room specially equipped for the course, where students can learn to access information and use slide-tape sequences. Literacy and numeracy are included in all modules, but in addition both are taught through individual withdrawal and there is an intensive counselling session each week.

It would be facile to suggest that such a course is free from problems. Some students are not only limited intellectually but also have social and emotional problems, and occasionally physical disabilities such as epilepsy. There may be need for extensive counselling with both students and their parents. Some are attention seeking, while integration in the college community is not easy for students who come from a relatively small and sheltered school environment, and who for much of the week are taught together. The course is expensive in staff time and, as it grows, will need additional staff time as well as specialist remedial expertise with this age group**(5)**.

5
Curriculum and general education

The problem of general education

Until the late 1950's general education in the sixth form was regarded as the incidental spin-off of a specialist course or specific preparation for Oxford and Cambridge scholarship examinations. Specialization, it was argued, ensured study in depth, coming to grips with the underlying discipline of the subject, from which it was appropriate to move out to consider wider issues. The general education of the Classical Sixth required not an injection of science or economics, but rather that the discipline of ancient languages and culture should be pursued to sufficient depth to make contact with the problems of the modern world. The exception to this was the acceptance that the Science Sixth needed some periods of English, history or French to complete their education.

It was perhaps C. P. Snow's Rede lecture, *The Two Cultures and the Scientific Revolution* (1958), bitterly criticized though it was, that opened the debate about the gap between scientific and literary culture and the contribution to this made by an over-specialized school curriculum. The Crowther Report, published in the following year, coined two phrases which found their way into the vocabulary of discussion of the sixth form curriculum. 'Minority time' described both complementary studies, balancing the main course of study and common elements taken by arts and science specialists together. The common element could, in Crowther's view, be summarized as 'religious education and all that goes to the formation of moral standards', art and music, and physical education. Alongside literacy for scientists, Crowther identified the need for 'numeracy' for the arts specialists. 'By numeracy,' he wrote, 'we mean not only the ability to reason quantitatively but also an understanding of scientific method and some acquaintance with the achievements of science.' Developments followed rapidly. Under the *Agreement to Broaden the Curriculum* (1961), 360 heads of schools undertook to devote at least one third of the sixth form curriculum to non-specialist studies and to avoid specialization before the sixth form was reached. The foundation of the General Studies Association in 1962 and the inclusion of a subject committee for General Studies when the Schools Council was formed in 1964, were landmarks in the arrival of a new area of the curriculum which gradually made an impact on the sixth form in the late 1960's. The

General Studies Association was able to report that 60% of all the schools it surveyed in 1974-75 had a common core to their sixth form curriculum and that a further 10% thought one was desirable**(19)**.

Idea and reality, however, have remained far apart. Few teachers and even fewer heads of schools and colleges are prepared to take a stand on the sufficiency of an exclusive diet of examination work, but the provision of general studies is rarely accorded high priority when scarce manpower resources are being allocated. The General Studies Association (1976) reported that 'a planned course of general studies is not the norm'. Schools Council Examinations Bulletin Number 38 (1978) concluded, 'By far the most common arrangement appears to be a programme which depends on the interests of and enthusiasms of teachers who are available to become involved once the other demands of the curriculum have been met.' A. D. C. Peterson, commenting pungently on the myths of the curriculum, concluded that non-specialist work did not occupy one third to one quarter of a sixth former's time as was claimed, nor did it form an important part of his education. The view that it did represented 'an emotional commitment to the protection of some loved but theoretical illusion.'**(34)** Part of the confusion arose from the assumption that some private study and homework time were allocated to general studies. In fact, both are overwhelmingly devoted to examination subjects. That student response to general studies is at best lukewarm is equally well documented in both the Schools Council Sixth Form survey of 1967 and the work of Dean, Choppin et al ten years later**(31,11)**.

The attitude of universities and employers is similarly ambivalent. Universities seek broadly educated students who display intellectual curiosity about all aspects of their work and are likely to contribute to the cultural, social and sporting life of the college. Personnel managers wish to recruit students who show adaptability, aptitude for team work, communications skills, in short what they refer to as 'the good generalist', rather than the 'narrow specialist'. In both cases, however, priority is accorded to high performance in A level examinations and in only marginal cases does evidence of general education carry much weight. The requirement to give details of the school's general studies programme and of the student's attitude towards it, was dropped from the UCCA form after a few years, as burdensome to record and superfluous to selection procedures.

Twenty years on from Crowther and the founding of the General Studies Association, the subject remains the Cinderella of the sixth form curriculum, so much so that many schools and colleges have dropped the name in the hope of improving the image. The problem is twofold. First, there is no agreed conceptual framework for the general work of the sixth form. There are plenty on offer but none approaches the coherence of the well established subject disciplines which dominate the curriculum. Second, most general studies programmes lack a goal. Crowther commented on the need for 'some sort of adventitious incentive' and much progress has been made where general studies has been examined. A non-examined area of the curriculum is no doubt a desirable objective. While, however, the most powerful drives are harnessed to an examined curriculum, this is simply not practicable. Students certainly derive motivation from the knowledge that they can acquire an examination qualification in general studies which may serve to compensate for a lapse in a specialist subject. In sixth form colleges, A level general studies is now the fourth most popular subject, taking its place after mathematics, English and physics.

Recent work on the secondary curriculum may yield a model not just for sixth form general education, but for the successful integration of specialist and general aspects of the education of the 16–19 age group. In *Curriculum 11–16* (1977), H. M. Inspectorate outlined the common curriculum for secondary schools as 'a body of skills, concepts, attitudes and knowledge' appropriate to the age and ability of the pupils. They identified eight areas of experience to which the curriculum would introduce pupils. These were:

the aesthetic and creative	the physical
the ethical	the scientific
the linguistic	the social and political
the mathematical	the spiritual

There have been a variety of similar categorizations. Schools Council Working Paper Number 45 (1972) listed eight elements in a balanced sixth form curriculum:

Communication skills	1	Literacy (and the related oracy)
	2	Numeracy
Knowledge and Understanding (cognitive)	3	A knowledge and understanding of man's natural and physical environment.
	4	A knowledge and understanding of man and his social environment.
Affective	5	A developing moral sensibility.
	6	A developing aesthetic sensibility.
Expressive	7	Fashioning the environment (the creative arts and the creative aspects of technology).
	8	Physical education in its widest sense.

The two facet model of the Crowther Report has thus become an eight facet model. It will, then, be the aim of the sixth form curriculum to introduce students to these areas of experience at an appropriate level and both specialist and general courses will make their contribution to its achievement.

The sixth form college in practice

We turn now to three models of general education currently in use in sixth form colleges.

General education as the core of the curriculum

Queen Mary's College, Basingstoke, has, from the beginning, placed general education in the forefront of the curriculum(**30,19**). Advanced level subjects receive four hours teaching each, while the general education programme is designated 'Main Studies', a title which the college describes as its 'most deliberate affront to general studies as minority time, a peripheral activity fitted into an uncongenial corner of the week'. All departments and all members of the staff contribute to the Main Studies programme of non-examination courses which are drawn up so that they require written work and background reading from all students. For some students whose examination programme is relatively light, Main Studies constitutes the larger part of their work in the college. For them, 'it is majority not minority time.' Since Main Studies is central to the comprehensive philosophy of the college, it is taught in mixed-ability groups with the Oxbridge aspirant rubbing shoulders with the new student who has scraped three or four low CSE grades. This in turn necessitates a variety of teaching methods and the devising of multimedia resources.

New College, Telford, sets out to give the same amount of attention to personal and social development that it devotes to the attainment of qualifications in public examinations. The timetable is in two parts: the Core Curriculum, whose object is personal development, and Electives (examination subject options), whose object is academic development. The Core Curriculum in which all participate includes tutor group, year group and college assembly, clubs and societies, an activities afternoon and physical education for all. At its heart, however, is Core Studies to which almost three hours per week are devoted by all. There is a deliberately wide overall theme, for example, 'The Development of Western Civilization'. There is a weekly lecture by a member of staff, delivered to each year group, with the second year taking similar themes but attending lectures of greater depth than those which the students will have heard the year before. There is a period when the tutor follows up the lecture with his tutor group or leads a discussion on a previously prepared alternative topic. A further period is spent on a modular course, lasting six weeks, which explores aspects of the theme in greater depth. Topics include the role of women in society, thinking about television, drugs, art and advertising in the twentieth century, and what is happening to our weather? The organization is in the hands of a vice-principal, with two teams of staff, one for arts and social studies, and one for science and technology. All students write two essays of 1500–2000 words each year and all have the opportunity to take the JMB General Studies at O or A level. The essays can be submitted as part of the course work required of an A level candidate (**47**).

General education through an examined course for all

Stoke on Trent S. F. College is unusual in having a department wholly concerned with the provision of the college's general studies programme. The seven staff of the department include members whose academic disciplines are theology and philosophy, history, English and music, the visual arts, mathematics and philosophy, together with a scientist with a technical bias and an interest in film. The main requirement, however, is not a specific academic area, but a desire to undertake the general education of students in the college. The programme followed by all students consists of:

Careers education	one period each week for one year
General English	two periods each week
Games	two periods each week
General Studies	three periods each week
Mathematics and Foreign Language	one period each week of each for those whose examination programme does not include them

The second unusual element in the programme at Stoke is that all students take an external examination, either A level or O level General Studies, or CEE in Contemporary Issues including oral and course work. Students are selected for the appropriate examination on entry to the college in the light of their external examination results and internal tests. One member of the general studies department is responsible for the group of students for their whole course, teaching them for three periods each week in the first year and for one period in the second. The syllabus is adapted from time to time but contains such modules as:

Man in society—roles, stereotypes, education, urbanization
Social problems—poverty, wealth, crime, stress, drugs, the disabled
Political institutions—parliamentary democracy, the EEC, alternative political systems, dictatorship, human rights
The Third World—population, hunger and inequality
Moral issues—ethical standpoints, human rights, capital punishment
Computers
Current Affairs

In the second year the group remains with the same tutor for one period, during which the emphasis is on examination preparation and the completion of six extended essays, which are either inter-disciplinary or else on two scientific, two arts and two social science topics. The double period becomes a series of six week modules with a selected topic studied in detail. Examples might be inflation and unemployment, the social responsibility of the scientist, and the problems of Northern Ireland.

General education through modular courses

Most colleges provide an ambitious programme of courses with a considerable range of choice. Names vary and the time which students are required to spend on general studies varies. Some colleges include a compulsory core course for all or part of the college. In others the whole programme is based on a free choice from a wide variety of courses though there may well be an obligation to discuss with the group tutor the options to be selected. In yet others, an attempt is made to ensure balance by specifying certain categories from which students must make their selection.

In few colleges is physical education compulsory; in most some form of physical recreation is expected. The emphasis is no longer on team games but on individual and small group sports, a preparation for sport in adult life stressing its recreative aspect. Few colleges have the staff or facilities to confine physical activities to Wednesday afternoon which is, however, often reserved for team fixtures. Activities abound from archery to yoga, horseriding to rockclimbing, some involving the local sports centre or specialist facilities such as the Calshot Activities Centre, used extensively by the Hampshire colleges. Craft, design and technology and home economics departments also make a significant contribution to the recreational aspect of the programme, building skills valuable in later life. Many courses are open ended, leading beyond the college to participation in a business game, a public speaking competition or a youth leadership course. The programme may also include workshop sessions enabling students to obtain staff help for individual problems, particularly in English and mathematics.

Despite the value of the work done in these voluntary courses, this area of the curriculum is not entirely a success story. The recreational courses are often the most successful, while those which require academic work inside and outside the classroom, such as learning a new modern language, are less well subscribed and liable to a high drop-out rate. The same is true of any academic course placed in competition with one which is less demanding. The shine may even wear off a recreational course if it occurs outside in inclement weather or takes place last period in the afternoon. Taster courses often lack depth, omitting skills and concepts in the interests of the immediately attractive.

Learning to learn

Like much else in the sixth form curriculum, study and learning skills have been assumed rather than taught. Students, it was believed, would

Curriculum and general education

General education programmes in four colleges

College	Solihull S. F. College
Title	Foundation Studies
Time	4 hours (2 hours physical recreation in addition) 2 courses of two hours each week. Half year, one year or two year courses available.
Categories	C Creative activities H Humanitites S Social science P Physical sciences
Notes	1. Students required to take one course in each category in which they are not taking an A level subject. 2. General Studies A level and General Paper O level (J.M.B.) available. Foundation studies provides preparation. 3. Occasional college lectures with follow-up seminars in tutor group. 4. O level repeat course may replace one course for half year.
College	Hereford S. F. College
Title	Liberal Studies
Time	4 hours
Categories	Recreations and community activities (2 hours)—sport, art, music, social service, practical skills. General Studies (1 hour)—essay writing and work on topics of general interest. Short courses (1 hour)—five week courses chosen from 30 available, alternating with general periods devoted to films, discussions and careers advice.
Notes	1. General Studies A level (London) is a main subject with modules on Science and Society and the Modern Movement. 2. All students enter for AO General Studies (Cambridge) after the two year course.
College	John Leggott College
Title	General Studies
Time	5 hours
Categories	1. One period each of physical education, general English, religious studies, games. 2. Statistics and computer application for all not taking A level in mathematics or geography. 3. General Studies courses: three in first year, two in second chosen from 60 options including philately, psychology, politics, campanology, folk dancing, machine embroidery.
Note	A level students take AO General Studies (Cambridge) after two years.
College	Itchen College
Time	$5\frac{1}{2}$ hours
Title and Categories	1. Humane Studies—two double periods in tutor groups a) Practical and creative activities—9 short courses introducing new activities e.g. pottery, drama, music, cookery, film making. b) General Studies—five short courses with emphasis on the contemporary world e.g. psychology, crime, politics, education. Religious education and human relations included for all. 2. Physical education and recreational activities—double period. 3. Careers—1 period each week in first year; lectures, films with ten options available each week.

Recreations timetable at South East Essex S.F. College

	9.00	9.40	10.20	11.55	12.10	2.30	3.10	3.50	4.30
Mon.				Basketball (mixed)	Badminton		Weight training Fitness training	Soccer club training	
Tues.	Judo Badminton			Five-a-side Soccer	Gymnastics Trampoline		Five-a-side Soccer	Rugby club training	
Wed.	Voluntary worship	Judo Badminton		General recreation	Badminton Cross-country Hockey Orienteering	College team fixtures Netball Riding Rugby	Soccer Squash	Badminton club	
Thurs.		Judo		General recreation	Indoor hockey Netball		Squash Tennis	Basketball club	
Fri.	Judo Badminton			General recreation	Gymnastics Trampoline		Volleyball		

Table tennis throughout the week by arrangement. Swimming at Runnymede pool at concessionary rates.
Note Times for Wednesday can be found on the timetable page 59.

learn by trial and error, while staff familiar with them would detect problems and remedy them. The arrival of the sixth form college has coincided with the realization that study skills are hard to acquire and that much valuable time can be lost in attempting to do so without adequate guidance. In adjusting to a new environment and unfamiliar teachers, students may conceal learning problems which as a result remain undiagnosed and uncorrected. Nor are staff always aware how incomprehensible apparently obvious instructions may be. The fledgling sixth former has little idea what is meant by the exhortation to 'read round the subject'. Bibliographies in books used by sixth formers sometimes fail to distinguish between what the student might reasonably read and the esoteric source material used by the textbook writer in his research.

The case for training in study skills is easily made. The problem of organizing it is more difficult. Study skills are often regarded as subject-specific, a sociologist being unable to help a mathematician or a musician to help a geographer. Equally it is maintained that all staff cannot be expected to include study skills in their repertoire of tutorial expertise. There are a number of models on offer:

1. A study skills course conducted by tutors in the early weeks of the course and at intervals during the year. Revision is, for example, better introduced before the first internal examination.
2. A study skills emphasis in all departments in the early weeks of the course.
3. A study skills centre to which all students are directed at specific times in their course.
4. A study skills course for all in their first four weeks in the college, using general studies time before the main course begins and mobilizing a substantial part of the staff to teach it.

Some colleges issue a study skills booklet as a basis for work in tutorial periods. Advice, however imparted, needs to be supported by practice. Note-taking, the use of a library, organizing a work programme need a mixture of theory, practice and evaluation. Conversely, theoretical knowledge is also valuable: revision skills, for example, are based on the ways in which memory operates through understanding, application and motivation. The teaching of study skills is a field in which many staff welcome a college-based in-service course.

Religious education

Religious education, still theoretically a compulsory subject, usually forms part of the college's general education programme. The justification is far more than the statutory obligation. If religious education is to be regarded as complete at 16, understanding will remain at an immature level and the more complex issues will never be reached. The figure of Jesus for example, is often studied by children at an age when they cannot grasp the significance of the miracles or parables, the nature of his mission or the paradoxes of his life, death and resurrection. A similar case can be made for a study in the sixth form of modern religious thought or of the great world faiths now practised in Great Britain. The theoretical case may be a strong one, practice is more difficult. Nobody who has attempted to offer religious studies courses in the sixth form in recent years can be under any illusion about the extent of student indifference, if not hostility. Many colleges offer optional courses knowing that they will appeal only to a minority. Others require students to select one course each year under the general heading of 'Beliefs and Values'. The programme at Barton Peveril College, Eastleigh, appears in *Paths to Understanding*, the Hampshire Handbook to Religious Education[20]. Students take three courses during their first five terms in the college, each lasting one hour per week for a term and including written assignments. There is also a Youth Leadership course run in association with the Y.M.C.A. National Centre at Fairthorne Manor. The options in the Beliefs and Values courses are: options for living; Indian religion; the Bible, archaeology and modern study; modern problems; the artist's vision of life; Christianity today; the business of being human.

Careers education and work experience

In recent years the emphasis in careers work has shifted from guiding young people into their first job, towards more general preparation for entry to the world of work, helping them to find their own identity and to develop decision making skills. In one sense, the entire college programme is careers education. When West Park College, Sandwell, became associated with the Schools Council Industry project, each department was asked if it wished to be involved and those who did so included not only chemistry, economics and design but modern languages, English and mathematics.

Sixth form colleges have a major commitment to careers education and guidance and the head of careers is a key figure with an important coordinating and servicing role. He works closely, first, with the County Careers Service which provides an advice and interview programme. Inside the college the group tutor often plays an important part in careers education. The head of careers may provide units of material with such titles as Planning Your Future, The Employment Scene and Money Matters, for use in tutorial periods. The programme will certainly include an introduction to the careers library, while the tutor period will be an opportunity to advertise careers visits in lunch-time or after college by local firms and representatives of the professions.

Many colleges include a careers conference as a focus of their year's work. Itchen College begins the second year with a two day conference run along the lines of the Industrial Society's sixth form conferences, which has the incidental advantage of freeing many staff to interview new students. At Stoke-on-Trent S. F. College, a fourteen week careers programme for all culminates in a Careers Convention held in February. Later a Leavers' Conference is held after examinations, when former students return to discuss their first year in work or higher education. No doubt experience of unemployment will, in the interests of reality, now have to be added.

Work experience has grown in popularity in recent years and many colleges make it available to as many students as possible. It involves two or three weeks during the course, though one week is often taken out of half term or a college holiday. Solihull S. F. College places almost 200 students on work experience in early July when there is probably least disruption to their work. Some colleges offer work experience for half a day a week coinciding with private study on the student's timetable. Work experience ideally offers a first hand introduction to working life. It involves the completion of an application form and the writing of a report when it is over. Students may encounter health and safety legislation and demarcation agreements as well as industrial relations issues. It involves the college in a great deal of work in arranging suitable placements and in visits while the students are out. There may, too, be a shortage of placements nearby, particularly where the local schools also have an ambitious programme of work experience.

Finally, entry to higher education is a year-round commitment. Even before the last polytechnic application has been posted, new students must be introduced to the complexities of UCCA. Advice on what to read and where to read it is highly complex. Some colleges appoint a member of each major department to advise students entering higher education on their subject area, leaving the head of careers to advise on psychology and archaeology and other subjects not likely to be covered by a department in the college. This is a further area where a day conference may be valuable, using films, visiting speakers and former students, and sometimes including a session in the evening to which parents are invited.

6
The college programme

The framework of the day

The day to day life of a school or college is determined by the structure of its working day and the timetable which arises from it. Yet both are the result of conventions and constraints which are rarely analysed and only acknowledged when they are called in question. As a new institution, it might be thought that the sixth form college would be free to go back to first principles and construct a framework appropriate to the needs of 16–19 year olds, rather than accept the limitations within which secondary schools operate. This has not, however, happened. Most sixth form colleges operate with a programme which is, with slight modifications, that operated by the schools from which they originated. There are two reasons for this. In the first place most, though not all, sixth form colleges evolve over five years, usually from a grammar school, and the needs of the old institution determine the framework of the new. By the time the college has fully emerged the mould is set. Second, colleges operate under Schools Regulations and there is therefore no provision for a three session day or for time off in lieu for staff. There is no tradition of an extended day, nor has a distinction been drawn between the framework within which the college operates, and the hours during which the staff are required to teach and staff and students are required to be on the premises.

A few colleges have broken out of the straitjacket. Hereford S.F. College, Tynemouth College, North Shields and King James's College of Henley are among those which have extended their day, though none beyond 4.45 p.m. South East Essex S.F. College operates a continuous day extending from 9.0 a.m. to 4.30 p.m. with a 15 minute tutorial period from 11.55 to 12.10 and staggered breaks and lunchtimes, making a total of 33 hours in the week. Havant College runs some minority courses after college hours and the college library is open for students from 7.30 a.m. to 6 p.m.

Timetable periods also resemble those of school. There is a preference for 40–45 minutes as the normal module, though a number of colleges use a 50–60 minute period length. Among less usual patterns, Farnborough College divides its day into three periods each lasting 95 minutes, while Bilborough College, Nottingham, has four periods each day varying

A four box timetable using a continuous day—South East Essex Sixth Form College

	9.00	9.40	10.20	11.55	12.10		2.30	3.10	3.50 4.30
Mon.	A1 1 Additional Maths. (O) 2 — 3 Mathematics (A)		B1 Geology (O) Economics (A) English (A)		C1 Physical Science (CEE) English (A) Lunch	C1 Lunch Lunch —	D1 Geography (O) American Studies (O) Economics (A)	D1 Geography (O) Additional Maths (O) Mathematics (A)	College meetings A1 — — —
Tues.	B2 1 Geology (O) 2 Economics (A) 3 English (A)		C2 Physical Science (CEE) English (A)		D2 Silversmithing (CEE) Lunch —	D2 Lunch Film and Communication (NE)	A2 Additional Maths (O) Mathematics (A)	A2 Additional Maths (O) Mathematics (O)	A1 — — —
Wed.		9.30 D1 Voluntary 1 Geography (O) Worship 2 American Studies (O) 3 Economics (A)	10.10 10.50 D1 A1 — — — — — — Mathematics (A)	A1 — —	12.15 Lunch	12.30 1.30 — — — — — —	2.30 — — Badminton (NE)	3.30	
Thurs.	C1 1 Physical Sciences (CEE) 2 English (A) 3 —		D1 American Studies (O) Economics (A)		A2 — Aspects of Politics (NE) Art (NE)	A2 Lunch Lunch	B1 Geology (O) Economics (A) English (A)	B1 Geology (O) Economics (A)	B2 — Basket- ball (NE)
Fri.	D2 1 Silversmithing (CEE) 2 — 3 Economics (A)		A2 Additional Maths (O) Mathematics (O) Mathematics (A)		B2 Geology (O) Economics (A) English (A)	B2 Lunch Lunch Lunch	C2 Physical Sciences (O) English (A) —	C2 Physical Sciences (O) — —	C1 — — —

Note 1. Numbers **1, 2, 3** above refer to the student programmes on page 60.
2. Dashes above indicate periods of private study.

1. 10.30–11.55 double period to include 15 minutes break taken before, during or after the period.
2. 11.55–12.10 (12.15–12.30 on Wednesday) tutorial period.
3. 12.10–2.30 (except Wednesday) double period to include 40 minute break, during or after the period.
4. Wednesday from 12.30–3.30 three periods which may be used for competitive games or for special paper periods.
5. Students attend lessons for a minimum of 30 periods in the first year, 28 in the second year. The notional length of the working week is 35 out of 40 periods.

Student timetables: some examples

First student Subject	level	periods	Second student Subject	level	periods	Third student Subject	level	periods
Additional Mathematics	O	6	Economics	A	8	Mathematics	A	8
Geology	O	8	English	A	8	English	A	8
Physical Science	C	8	American Studies	O	6	Economics	A	8
Geography	O	8	Mathematics	O	4	Art	NE	2
Silversmithing	C	4	Film and Communication	NE	2	Badminton	NE	2
			Aspects of Politics	NE	2	Basketball	NE	1

NE = non-examination course   C = Certificate of Extended Education

Time	Box	Monday		Tuesday		Wednesday		Thursday		Friday	
		Assembly		Core Studies		Tutorial		Core Studies		Core Studies	
9	a	B b1	P S			B b1	Law				Lecture or
	b		b1	D d1	P S		b2	A a1	English		tutorial
	c		b2		d1		b2		a1	C c1	Mathematics
10	a		b2		d2	Political Studies	A a2		a2	P S		c1
	b		b2		d2		a2		a2		c2
	c	C c1	Mathematics	A a1	English	C c1	Mathematics	D d1			c2
11	a		c1		a1		c1		d1	B b1	Law
	b		c2		a2	P S	D d2	P S		d2	Political Studies		b1
	c		c2		a2		d2	Political Studies		d2		b2
12	a		c2		a2		d2		d2		b2
	b										
1	b	D d1	P S	C c1	Mathematics			B b1	Law	A a2	P S
	c		d1		c1		Activities		b1		a2
2	a		d1		c1		afternoon		b1		a2
	b		d2	Political Studies		c2			b2	P S		a1	English
	c		d2		c2				b2		a1
3	a	A a1	English	B b1	Law			C c2		D d1	P S
	b		a1		b1				c2		d1
	c		a1		b1				c2		d1

1. Each box contains 19 or 20 modules divided 9 and 10 or 10 and 10 between half boxes.
2. The college day runs from 8.50 a.m. to 4.00 p.m. with a 40 minute break for lunch.
3. PS = Private study.

Student Timetable

Subject	level	box	modules	hours
English	O	a1	9	3
Law	A	B	15	5
Mathematics	A	C	16	5 1/3
Political Studies	O	d1	9	3
Core Studies		—	7	2 1/3
Tutorial		—	1	1/3
Assembly		—	1	1/3

A four box timetable using modules of varied length—Bilborough College, Nottingham

	9.00		9.20		11.10	12.30		1.50	3.00
Mon.	TG		1 90	Break	Common studies 80		TG	3 70	2 60
Tues.	TG	AA	2 90		1 80		TG	4 70	3 60
Wed.	TG / VW		4 90		3 80			Activities 90	
Thurs.	TG		3 90		4 80		TG	2 70	1 60
Fri.	TG	CA	Common studies 90		2 80		TG	1 70	4 60

1. Length of periods indicated in minutes (90, 80, 70, 60).
2. Wednesday activities occupy a notional 90 minutes.
3. Common studies coupled with boxes 1 & 2 to tie in with Foundation course students on link courses.
4. 75 minutes for lunch to enable voluntary societies and activities to take place.
5. TG = Tutor Group.
6. AA = Admin. Assembly.
7. VW = Voluntary Worship.
8. CA = College Assembly.
9. Break is 20 minutes long (from 10.50–11.10).
10. Afternoon Tutor Group is from 1.45–1.50.

A five box timetable using 60 and 90 minute modules

Period	Time	Mon.	Tues.	Wed.	Thurs.	Fri.
1	9.10–10.10	C French	E P.S.	E P.S.	C French	A P.S.
2	10.10–11.10	B English	10.40 Tutorial	D Sociology	10.40 Tutorial	E Science in Society (N.E.)
3	11.30–1.00	A Metalwork (N.E.)	B English	C French	E P.S.	D Sociology
4	2.00–3.00	D Sociology	C French	A 1st XI Football	A P.S.	B English
5	3.00–4.00	3.30 Meetings	D Sociology	3.30	B English	3.30

1. Registration 9.00–9.10 daily. Tutorial includes careers education and counselling and occasional assemblies for a section of the college.
2. Each box has $2 \times 1\frac{1}{2}$ and 2×1 hour periods.
3. Home Economics, Art, Design Technology etc can be timetabled across boxes AB and CD to allow longer periods for practical work.
4. P.S. = Private study.   5.   N.E. = Non-examined.

Student timetable

Subject	level	hours	box
English	A	5	B
French	A	5	C
Sociology	A	5	D
Football	NE	$1\frac{1}{2}$	A
Metalwork	NE	$1\frac{1}{2}$	A
Science in Society	NE	1	E
Private study	—	6	AE

between 70 and 90 minutes in length. The problem is that of reconciling the needs of different subjects, levels and teaching styles. Those taking science, craft, design and technology, and home economics prefer longer periods while those teaching arts subjects prefer shorter periods. Advanced level candidates can use longer periods, while students on some other courses are better suited by shorter and more frequent periods.

This problem is hard to solve within the confines of the normal school day. Single periods of 45 minutes are too short and double periods of 90 minutes are too long for some. New College, Telford, operates a timetable using 20 minute modules, with no fixed break in the morning, and with only 40 minutes for lunch shared by the whole college, though extended at either end for a proportion of students and staff. The result is a framework of 30 hours. Havant College has a timetable with 14 hour-long periods and 8 periods of 90 minutes, allowing a framework of 26 hours.

The box structure

Ever since the Arts and Science Sixth, with their separate timetables, disappeared from the grammar school sixth form, a box structure has been used as a framework for choice of main subjects. A number of sets in each subject allows them to be placed in different boxes to facilitate greater choice. The majority of sixth form colleges use a four box structure, though Wednesday afternoon is often reserved for games and recreational activities. For A level students this arrangement works well. General studies, ancillary courses and private study may take place in the fourth box or be part of each box. For one year students it is less satisfactory. A four subject programme does not provide a sufficiently demanding programme for all one year students though it may meet the needs of some. Five or six subjects are preferable and the CEE was designed to be taken in five subjects. One solution is to allocate half a box to all or some one year subjects, thus allowing a programme of six subjects, as well as a free box for non-examination work. This may, however, produce inadequate contact time for candidates who are either attempting a new subject or who need help to master the skills which have so far eluded them. Other solutions have been adopted. First, some allocate a full box to more demanding one year subjects and half a box to others. Second, the one year course may be timetabled quite separately and outside the boxes used for A level students. This may prove to be quite a difficult operation since staff have then to be fitted into two different patterns. Third, some colleges extend the time available in each box so that two one year courses can each receive sufficient contact time. A final solution is to adopt a five box model in which the fifth box may have a smaller time allocation and is used for a restricted range of subjects.

	2 Year	TWO YEAR COURSES. Choose your subjects from THREE of the columns OR, for Secretarial Course, from FOUR columns.			
		A	B	C	D
'A' Level Courses		Biology Computer Studies Craft: Design & Practice (Fabric Printing, Lettering, Sculpture) Design Economics Engineering Science English Literature Fashion and Fabrics Geography Mathematics Physics Pure Mathematics with Statistics Religious Studies Russian	Art British Government & Politics Economics Engineering Science Further Mathematics Geology Geometrical & Engineering Drawing History Home Economics Latin Mathematics Physics Physics & Mathematics Pure Mathematics with Statistics	Biology Chemistry Computer Studies Craft: Design & Practice (Pottery, Print Making) English Literature French Geography Mathematics (for Further Mathematics Students only) Religious Studies	Art British Government & Politics Chemistry Classical Civilization English Literature French Geology Geometrical & Engineering Drawing German History Home Economics Mathematics Music Pure Mathematics with Statistics Spanish Woodwork
3 Year Course		Russian	German		
Secretarial Course		Typing & Secretarial Duties	Shorthand	Shorthand	Typing & Secretarial Duties
Special Course		Physical Education			
AO/O Levels		Additional Mathematics	Additional Mathematics	X: American Studies, Drama & Theatre Arts, Human Biology, Physics, Religious Studies / Y: Additional English, Applied Geography, Chemistry, Electronics, Music	
				Spanish	
1 Year		ONE YEAR COURSES: Choose ONE subject from each of columns B, C and D			
		A	B	C	D
CEE		Communication Contemporary Issues	Economics French Studies Geography History Politics and Local Community Religious Studies	Art Craft Technology Creative Fashion Studies Drama & Theatre Arts Music Physical Science	Geology Mathematics Social Biology

Subject option scheme at South East Essex Sixth Form College

	A		B	
A Level	Art Biology (9) Business Studies Chemistry (9) Computer Science Economics English French Geography History Music Physics (9) Psychology Sociology		Art Biology (9) Social Biology Chemistry (9) Computer Science Economics Electronic Systems English Geography Geometrical and Machine Drawing German History Music Physics (9) Politics and World Affairs Practical Music Religious Studies	
AO Two Year Course				
AO and O One Year Course	Human Biology Chemistry Geology Physics Technology		Human Biology Chemistry Economics Geology Religious Studies	
	a1	a2	b1	b2
	Biology English Language English Literature Geometrical and Machine Drawing German Mathematics Sociology Statistics	Additional Mathematics (6) English Literature Geography (6) History (6) Mathematics (5)	Additional Mathematics English Language English Literature French Mathematics Physics Sociology	English Language Mathematics Metalwork
CEE	Electricity and Electronics		Art Mathematics Silversmithing	Art English History Geography Mathematics
	Art History Mathematics	Art Mathematics English		
FS	Foundation Studies			

C	D
ology (9) onomics glish ography story thematics sic ctical Music ssian eatre Studies anish	Art Biology (9) Design and Technology Economics English French Geography History Mathematics Politics and World Affairs Sociology
uble Mathematics (12) ecialist Mathematics (16)	
ssian	Spanish
iness Studies man Biology gious Studies	Drama Economics Geography (6) Human Biology Latin Physics

c1	c2	d1	d2
lish Language lish Literature ch hematics dy of Art odwork hematics for ysicists (NE)	Additional Mathematics (6) American Studies (6) English Literature Geography (6) Government and Politics (5) Mathematics (5)	Astronomy English Language English Literature History (5) Mathematics Photography Psychology Sociology	Additional Mathematics Chemistry English Language Government and Politics Physics
lish ory graphy hematics	Art Local Studies (5) English Mathematics	Art Mathematics Religious Studies Silversmithing	Art English Mathematics
	Applied Biology Physical Science		

ach box contains nine or ten periods. Whole box subjects are allocated eight periods except where otherwise dicated. Half box subjects are normally allocated four periods but may receive five or six periods.
ifferent syllabus within a subject and multiple sets in the same box are not indicated.

Subject option scheme at Hereford S.F. College

ADVANCED LEVEL SUBJECTS

1A	1B	1C	1D
Biology Chemistry Physics Mathematics Ancient History English Early Modern History Geography Government & Political Studies Economics French Spanish Needlework & Dressmaking I Design I General Studies	Biology Physics Further Mathematics Mathematics Religious Studies English Early Modern History Geography Latin Economics German Art I Home Economics I Communication Studies I	Biology Chemistry Physics Mathematics Computer Science English Modern History Geography Government & Political Studies Economics Russian Music Psychology Needlework & Dressmaking II Design II Physical Education Course	Biology Chemistry Geology Mathematics Computer Science English Modern History Medieval History Geography Economics French Art II Home Economics II Communication Studies II

ORDINARY LEVEL SUBJECTS

1A(i)	1A(ii)	1B(i)	1B(ii)	1C(i)	1C(ii)	1D(i)	1D(ii)
English Language Political Studies	Mathematics Environmental Studies	Chemistry Commercial Mathematics Latin Music	AO Social Biology Mathematics English Language Spanish	Mathematics Archaeology French	Biology French	English Language Economic and Public Affairs Russian	Physics History German Electronics
1A(iii)		1B(iii)		1C(iii)			
Sociology		Art		Geology			

1. Advanced level candidates in home economics, needlework and dressmaking, communication studies and design follow courses 1 & 2 in the subject. (The subjects are timetabled across two boxes.)
2. Students who have taken CSE rather than O level in science or mathematics have an additional one or two hours teaching in the first year.
3. Students who wish to take chemistry at A level but who have not taken it at O level may do so provided they have a good record in physics and mathematics. Enrichment lessons are provided in the first year.

Subject option scheme at Eccles College, Salford

A	B	C	D	E
A English	A English	A English	A/*Interest*	General Studies
Geography	French	French	Business Studies	
History	German	Geography	Further Maths	5 courses are
French	Spanish	History		chosen from 40
Art	Economics	Economics	*Post O 1 year*	
Mathematics	Sociology	Mathematics	French for Business	European Studies
Pure Mathematics	Geology	Pure Mathematics	German for Business	
Physics	Art	Mathematics with		In second year:
Chemistry	Music	Statistics	O/*Interest*	
Biology	Mathematics	Further	Drama	Pre-teacher training
	Mathematics with	Mathematics	Horticulture	course
	Statistics	Physics	Art	
	Physics	Chemistry		German for
	Biology	Social Biology	O	Scientists
	Social Biology		Music	Photography
			Family Economics	
			Computer Studies	
O Human Biology	O History	O English Literature		
Geography	Religious Studies	Art	*O repeat (year)*	
Chemistry	Economics	Physics	English	
Art	Art	Biology	Physics	
	Family and	Geology	Chemistry	
	Community		Biology	
			German	
			French	
CEE English	CEE English	CEE Mathematics	Mathematics	
Mathematics	Mathematics			
Human			*O (two year)*	
Biology			Sociology	
			Spanish	
			German	
			Latin	
			Russian	
			Electronics	
			Interest (1/2 years)	
			Mathematics for	
			Physics	
			Environmental	
			Studies	
			German	
			Physical Activities	
			Ceramics	
			Latin	
			CEE	
			Mathematics	
			Environmental	
			Studies	

Students select their main course from columns A, B and C. Columns D and E are completed when they enter the college in September.
Three patterns of study are available:
One year pattern 3 O/CEE
Two year pattern 1 A + 4/5 O/CEE
  2 A + 2/3 O/CEE
  3 A + possible 1 O
  Up to 7 O/CEE taken over two years
One plus two year pattern First year is used to qualify for entry to a desired A level subject whilst taking a mixture of A, O and CEE subjects.

The student programme

Some students enter the college with eight or nine O levels at grade A, others have taken no external examination at school and there is every variety in between. All will have been placed provisionally on an appropriate course when they were interviewed early in the year. In many cases further counselling will be needed in September before their course is settled. The final stage is to decide the details of their timetable after discussion about recreational and general education courses which they will be taking.

Course options in a sixth form college related to qualifications on entry.

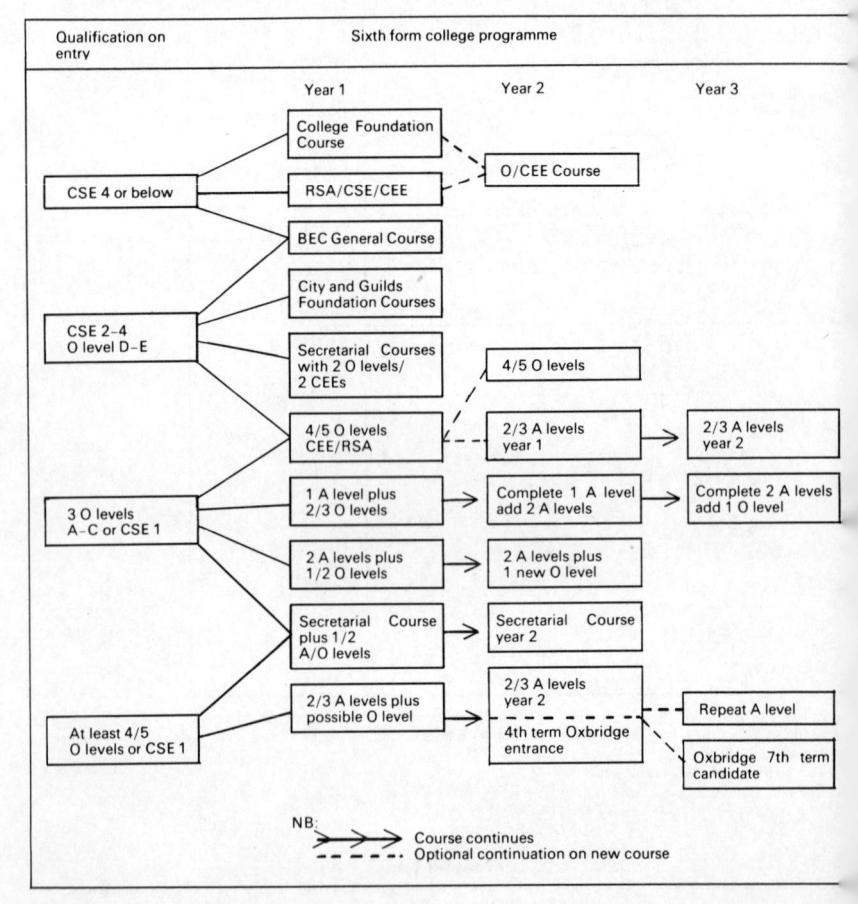

Qualification on entry	Sixth form college programme		
	Year 1	Year 2	Year 3
CSE 4 or below	College Foundation Course		
	RSA/CSE/CEE	O/CEE Course	
	BEC General Course		
CSE 2–4 O level D–E	City and Guilds Foundation Courses		
	Secretarial Courses with 2 O levels/ 2 CEEs	4/5 O levels	
	4/5 O levels CEE/RSA	2/3 A levels year 1	2/3 A levels year 2
3 O levels A–C or CSE 1	1 A level plus 2/3 O levels	Complete 1 A level add 2 A levels	Complete 2 A levels add 1 O level
	2 A levels plus 1/2 O levels	2 A levels plus 1 new O level	
	Secretarial Course plus 1/2 A/O levels	Secretarial Course year 2	
At least 4/5 O levels or CSE 1	2/3 A levels plus possible O level	2/3 A levels year 2 / 4th term Oxbridge entrance	Repeat A level / Oxbridge 7th term candidate

NB:
⟶ Course continues
- - - - Optional continuation on new course

Two year courses
The two year student's programme is likely to include two or three A level subjects, each of which is normally allocated about 5 hours teaching. Few colleges allow less than $4\frac{1}{2}$ hours, though Queen Mary's College, Basingstoke, has from the beginning accorded a key place to its Main Studies, and A level subjects receive 4 hours of teaching each. There is some research evidence to suggest that contact time in excess of 4 hours has no influence on examination results(**7**). Most colleges feel, however, that there should be time for work with individuals and small groups and that $4\frac{1}{2}$ to 5 hours is the optimum if this is to happen. Students taking less than three A levels are likely, instead, to be taking one or two O level or CEE subjects. The total time allocated to examination subjects is likely to be 14–16 hours. There will probably be about 5 hours private study in the student's timetable. The remaining 5 hours will be used in a variety of ways. A small but growing proportion of students take four A levels. For some, these may be mathematics, further mathematics, physics and chemistry, though this is a programme which leaves disturbingly little time for general education and recreational activities. If there are to be four A levels, then the fourth should represent a contrasting subject discipline. A student able to take A level music alongside sciences or social sciences is no doubt a rarity but is not unknown. A/O or CEE subjects such as archaeology, psychology, pottery or home economics may be less demanding academically than a fourth A level, while still providing a valuable balance to the student's timetable. General studies taken as a fourth A level or O level subject frequently provides a framework for a balanced programme of general courses as well as an incentive for written work.

One year courses
Students coming to the college for a one year course may constitute as many as half of the total entry. They come for the most part for a further year of general education, often to retrieve past failure, and some are seeking a firmer foundation on which to build a two year A level course subsequently. Success, however, is not easy to achieve. Many colleges now allow as much contact time for O level and CEE subjects as they do for A level, usually 4–5 hours. The number of subjects is usually five, sometimes six or four. The examination course will total 20 hours, leaving rather less time for other courses than is the case with two year students. They will, however, probably be allocated less private study time. Some colleges provide a compulsory core course for their one year students including perhaps, careers education, learning skills, health education and computer appreciation.

Some one year courses are complete in themselves. The City and Guilds Foundation Courses, for example, include general and careers education components. There is, however, still an opportunity to join in the college's sporting and recreational as well as extra-curricular activities.

A one year course based on O level and CEE—Havant College.

Main studies—four O level or CEE subjects including English and Mathematics unless already passed at O level grade C or CSE grade 1	20 hours
Core studies—five elements taken during the year 1 Health 2 Political education or current affairs 3 The world of work or drama and media studies 4 Study skills 5 Computer appreciation	1 hour
Other optional courses 1 A fifth examined O or CEE subject for recommended students only, who are exempted from core studies 2 Main studies physical education course with options in water survival, human measurement and performance and fitness for work 3 Support studies to improve basic skills in English and mathematics 4 Games 5 Non-examination courses in art, music, physical education, sailing and photography 6 Community service	at least 2 hours

The college meeting

School assembly has in recent years come under attack from a number of quarters. The secularization of society has for many people made a daily meeting for prayer a glaring anachronism, while compulsion is contrary to the spirit of worship. If instead, the assembly is a celebration of shared values, then daily may be too often and assembly an artificial medium to do it effectively. Sixth form colleges start with a further problem. In the minds of students, assembly is reminiscent in name, time and style of the school they have just left and in their view assembly is unsuited to their new status as students. It is therefore surprising that so many colleges have retained an assembly. The Education Act of 1944 which specifies a daily act of worship applies to all institutions run under Schools Regulations. More important than any legal obligation, however, is the value colleges attach to their community heritage. The college which meets together stays together. It is, moreover, the one occasion when the principal can meet the college and he is reluctant to forego this and take a further step towards becoming an administrator on the technical college model.

If a college meeting is desirable its name, nature, timing and function need to be adjusted to the new institution. 'College meeting' gets away from the name associated with school. In most colleges with over 500 students, only a section of the college can in any event meet at one time. Surprisingly few colleges use senior tutor groups. The reason appears to be that they are arbitrary groupings and neither exist long enough nor have sufficient in common, to acquire the cohesion associated with the year group or the house in the secondary school. There is a move away from 9 a.m. Many colleges meet before break in the morning or before lunch. Some colleges have one or two half hour tutor periods each week which can be used for a college or section meeting, either on a regular pattern or when occasion requires one. Queen Mary's College, Basingstoke, holds a weekly College Hour when staff and students meet for some form of shared experience—drama, music, poetry, a visiting speaker, a student panel or debate. In few colleges is the content of the college meeting exclusively religious. Many colleges characterize their meeting as religious, philosophical, ethical and moral as well as administrative and social. In some colleges students make a regular contribution. At New College, Telford, the choice of theme is the responsibility of a tutor group in turn. For some colleges the meeting is a special occasion held perhaps twice a term—the beginning of the college year, Remembrance Day, Christmas, the end of the sports festival and a post-examination leaving day, for example.

Some colleges have broken away entirely from the school assembly model, preferring instead a small group pattern. They rely on drama, music, games and social gatherings in which staff and students share, to create a sense of community. Many principals have come to recognize that it is unproductive or even counter-productive to be seen by students in the authoritarian role associated with presiding at college assembly.

About a quarter of the colleges make provision for voluntary worship, some weekly, one or two twice a week, and others once a month. Those with a religious tradition or foundation may hold a college Communion Service.

Work assignments

The issue of private study further illustrates the ambivalence felt by college staff about their responsibility to parents and students, and by students about the degree of freedom accorded to them. The school tradition is one of full-time education, with the day spent on the premises and the expectation of games and societies during lunchtime and after school. Some sixth form students resent any such expectations, feeling them to be incompatible with approaching adulthood and with the exhortation of the college to organize their own work. Many argue that their own home or the local library offers better facilities for quiet study than an over-crowded study room or the college common room. They feel it inconsistent with the dignity of a sixteen year old, still more an eighteen year old, that they should arrive for registration at 9 a.m. if their first lesson is not until 10 a.m. The college may be less sure that the sixteen year old can handle such a sudden change of regime. There are also legal obligations as well as responsibility to parents, not all of whom may welcome a son or daughter's erratic daily programme.

Of the sixty five colleges contributing to *Organisation of Sixth Form Colleges* (APVIC, 1981) thirty eight required all private study to be spent on the premises, while only a few gave complete freedom to all students to spend private study periods off the premises(1). The remainder offer a variety of gradations of freedom. Some make students spend all their private study in the college for the first term or half year and then let them leave after the last taught period but not before 2.30 p.m. During the second year, all private study may be spent off the premises. Another variant is to allow second year students to agree with their group tutor a division between free periods, which may be spent off the premises, and private study periods which are to be spent on college premises. The former may be a maximum of five hours in order to discourage students from restricting their general studies choices in order to leave early. Some colleges allow home study on Wednesday afternoon for those students who are not occupied in the games programme.

A majority of colleges supervise private study, some rigorously with the full panoply of class registers and a silence rule, others less obtrusively by visits of duty or senior staff. Many colleges provide alternatives: a supervised silent study area and a more relaxed unsupervised quiet study room. ('Quiet' according to the principal of Ludlow College is the antonym of 'silent'.) This arrangement is popular with students, giving those who genuinely want to work the opportunity to do so, free from the oppressive atmosphere of compulsion. The supervision of private study is not popular with staff, and with staff reductions is probably becoming less frequent. Some colleges reject the supervision of private study on principle; it is contrary both to the spirit of post-compulsory education and to the style of learning for which the college stands.

Homework is another word with childhood associations and is therefore avoided by colleges. A quarter of colleges specify a recommended time to be devoted to A level work assignments; five hours for each subject in addition to private study, for example. During the first six weeks at Brockenhurst College, detailed work assignments to be undertaken outside lessons are issued to all students to accustom them to the idea of designing a pattern of work which suits them and planning it well in advance. At Peel College, Bury, advice on organizing work is given both in the Induction week and in the Study Methods Course.

Rules and Sanctions

College rules vary from a comprehensive compendium covering every eventuality to a brief guide exemplifying dependence on common sense and goodwill, with the second model preferred by most colleges. Skelmersdale College Handbook lists only three rules, though it states unequivocally that failure to observe them is likely to lead to exclusion from the college.

1 You must attend punctually every meeting of every class shown on your timetable.
2 You must attempt all homework and classwork set and produce it on time.
3 You must not damage or steal college property or the property of other members of the college.

There are, however, three issues apart from that of compulsory full-time attendance, which cause particular breast beating by colleges—smoking, alcohol and dress. Had smoking not been shown to be a major health hazard and early smoking likely to lead to addiction, the attempt to prohibit smoking in schools would probably by now have been abandoned. Since, however, both medical and public opinion are strongly opposed to smoking, schools and colleges feel obliged to attempt to enforce anti-smoking rules. New College, Telford, prohibits smoking, its rule stating: 'Smoking causes pollution, annoyance to non-smokers, is expensive and a danger to health. In view of these considerations we trust you will not be surprised to learn that the whole of the college buildings are no smoking areas.' Only about one third of colleges, however, attempt total prohibition. The remainder recognize that it will only be driven underground or just outside the college gate. A majority, therefore, bow to the inevitable and restrict smoking hours to non-academic periods of the day and specify where it may take place. These are frequently places whose description eloquently conveys disapproval or grudgingly the existence of vice: 'a small, cold, windowless common room', 'an external caged area', 'the forecourt of the social block', 'a specified common room fitted with an extractor fan'. One college allows smoking only with a letter of parental consent.

On the subject of alcohol the college has the law on its side, at least as far as those under eighteen are concerned. There is, however, a student view that what the law allows—the consumption of alcohol at eighteen—the college may not prohibit. Colleges do; as one college rule puts it laconically but accurately, 'study and alcohol do not mix'.

Conventional school uniform has been adopted by few colleges, though some are reluctant to abandon all control. Some specify trousers, shirt, tie and jacket for boys and proscribe denim jeans, while others set as their criterion 'what would be suitable for general office work'—another way of prohibiting jeans. A majority of colleges recognize that the ethos of the college is such as to make dress regulations anomalous. John Leggott College specifies only that clothes should be 'sensible and should not be flamboyant, vulgar, provocative, scruffy or dangerous', while South East Essex S.F. College 'welcomes elegant, colourful and tasteful dress and requires only that it shall be of design and material suitable for work in the college.' Palmers College, Grays, introduces a light touch: 'Sunbathing is not part of the college activities ... boys are not allowed to remove their shirts.'

In the view of some students, the end of compulsory schooling sees the end of punishment. Like other transitions this one also can be too abrupt. Not all students may be ready to pass from an imposed discipline, enforced by the threat of punishment, to self discipline with no sanctions. The aim of all colleges is to make self-discipline effective as early as possible. 'Personal influence, persuasion, gentle pressure', 'sanctions are verbal, we seek cooperation'—are ways of expressing this aspiration. There may then be only the final sanctions of parental interview, suspension and expulsion from the college. Other colleges find that the transition from school to college requires intermediate sanctions. Most problems are associated with poor standards of work, lateness for or absence from lessons, and disregard for the college rules on smoking or the consumption of alcohol. Intermediate sanctions include withdrawal of privileges connected with private study: D.P.S. (Directed Private Study, taking place in a study room supervised by staff), withdrawal of home study where this exists, 'academic probation' with a report from staff after a fortnight or a month, are examples. Some colleges prefer to operate only the natural and longer term sanctions of adult life: 'the reality of an honest reference', or the equal reality of a poor examination result. For unpunctuality there is the reminder that this is a question frequently asked by potential employers. Some students may be admitted to the college on academic probation, while others are reminded that progress to the second year is not automatic. King James's College of Henley operates a system of examination retakes, the first in July, with a final retake in September.

All colleges value contact with parents but this too depends in part on the cooperation of the students in taking reports and newsletters home. A full report on the student's progress is usually produced twice a year and there may be briefer assessments at more frequent intervals. Parents' evenings are held, students often accompanying their parents.

Finally, colleges request a contribution to the college club fund to be used for activities which the local authority does not finance. Team games, the college minibus, societies and clubs, the college magazine, come under this heading and the subscription varies from 50 pence to

£6 per year. Many colleges also require caution money, a deposit on books and locker keys. This ensures care of property and the return of books, as well as providing a modest income through the investment of the capital sum for the duration of the student's stay in the college.

The Student Council

The Student Council is an important part of the hidden curriculum of the college, its effectiveness a test of how far the college is able to make democratic processes work. The council needs to have a simple yet carefully thought-out constitution, covering its rights and responsibilities as well as the frequency and method of elections. There needs to be continuity of membership and officers, together with an opportunity for new students to be fully represented by half term in their first autumn term. The council and its executive should include members of the staff and have ready access to the principal, without feeling that freedom of discussion is inhibited. They should have responsibility for some part of the student subscription and an opportunity of presenting a budget to the council. There are problems encountered at one time or another by all such bodies. The council may become associated with one section of college life or opinion. It may be felt to devote too much energy to sport, social activities or social service. It may be afflicted by apathy or fall under the control of an activist clique, determined to wage war on college rules and customs. It may elect officers for their popularity rather than their competence. Students will, in any of these circumstances, be learning lessons of no mean value about the realities of democratic politics. Members of the council need consistent support from staff representatives. Officers require careful briefing, not only on their specific tasks, but on the mechanics of committee procedure, on how to chair a meeting, take minutes, accept resolutions and lead deputations.

7
From school to college

The short course comprehensive school

The great majority of students entering the college at sixteen are the product of what is sometimes called the short course comprehensive school, a convenient omnibus term for schools with an age span of 11–16, 12–16 and occasionally 13–16. Yet curiously little has been written about these schools. Their birth was grudging; Circular 10/65 stated baldly, 'At first sight the 11–16 school has few arguments to recommend it', while Benn and Simon described them as 'one of the most controversial of all types of comprehensive school'**(2)**. To some people they are the dark side of the divide at 16; the price which has to be paid for the economies of scale associated with the sixth form college.

At first sight short course comprehensive schools appear to differ from 11–18 schools largely by omission; they do not have a sixth form. This omission, however, alters the institution quite radically. The academic aspirations of the sixth form, the fact that its members have chosen to stay at school, together with the social priorities of the eighteen year old, exert an influence out of proportion to their relatively small number and this affects both staff and pupils. Their membership of 1st XV Rugby team and the Dramatic Society changes the nature of the club into something more serious and more adult. It is intangible feelings such as these which underlie the reservations felt within the teaching profession and most frequently voiced by those whose earlier experience lay in the 11–18 school.

Yet the reservations are not easy to substantiate, or to quantify. One of the few surveys of the short course comprehensive school was undertaken by the 11–16 panel of the Headmasters' Association in 1977 and published in the SHA *Review* in July 1979**(41)**. The views of 170 heads about staffing, curriculum and the general life of the school were collected. The claim is frequently made that 11/12–16 schools find staff recruitment a problem, an allegation which the Macfarlane Report repeated, though it produced no evidence to support it. Only 15% of heads in the survey reported difficulties, while 77% said they normally recruited staff of high quality and good experience. In 1977, 80% of applicants were considered satisfactory and specialist staff were appointed to fill 92% of the vacancies. Some subjects posed problems:

mathematics (in 43% of 168 schools), modern languages (39%), heavy craft and technical studies (33%), science and particularly physics (28%). Had a survey of 11–18 schools been undertaken at the same time it would almost certainly have produced a similar result and some would have added that their large size constituted one of the disincentives to applicants. The academic quality of staff is harder to measure, though the HMA survey showed a good proportion of graduates, particularly in the larger schools. It would be idle to deny that some academically well qualified staff seek only posts which hold out prospects of Advanced level work and contact with incipient scholars. It is equally a mistake to equate good teaching with highly qualified graduates. Good teaching has more to do with an individual's skill as a communicator, with originality, warmth of personality and interest in the pupils for their own sake. Nevertheless, the ablest pupils probably miss the academic edge imparted to work in the fourth and fifth form by a teacher whose battery of talents includes real scholarship. Some subjects only reach fruition in the sixth form. Some linguists claim, for example, that a break-through to fluency is helped by knowing that there are students taking part in a French play or a foreign exchange and reading 'real' literature which never comes to those who stop at O level. It could certainly be argued that a break at 16 is more damaging in modern languages than it is in some other subjects. It is claimed that in other subjects the 11–16 school misses the A level perspective which the top sets in the 11–18 school may have, unless understanding between the college and its contributory schools is particularly close.

The HMA survey does not support the charge of curriculum impoverishment. All but two schools were offering French and 70% of the larger ones (700 plus) German too, while 31 taught Latin and 24 Spanish. 142 were able to provide separate sciences, while special help for slow learners was available in most. Size appears to be an important consideration. A six form entry, producing a roll in an 11–16 school of about 900 with a staff of 45, is likely to be viable and allow some flexibility for falling rolls. Once the staff drops to 35 the protection of the curriculum becomes a serious problem and the provision of specialist courses in science and languages and to meet remedial needs is difficult. The 12–16 school, with one year less to establish its courses before options are needed, is in respect of curriculum altogether more vulnerable. In the future the adoption of a core curriculum with fewer choices and more common elements may overcome some of the problems of a break at 16 and provide a common starting point for post-16 provision, whether it takes place in school, sixth form or tertiary college, or in further education.

The overall view of the short course comprehensive school may depend on its stage of development. The decapitated school with its senior pupils and more ambitious staff withdrawn, its status apparently diminished and Burnham group reduced, will probably be demoralized and find it hard to see advantages in its new role. The planned 11-16 school may value its homogeneity, develop a strong *esprit* and give fifth form pupils who do not intend to continue in full-time education beyond the age of sixteen responsibility and opportunities for leadership. It may be a community school in a real sense, with strong links with town or village and reduced travel problems for its pupils. Finally, it may be able to give dispassionate advice to its leavers on careers and further education, free from the obligation to build its own sixth form.

Liaison between school and college

When first conceived, the 11/12-16 school and the sixth form college were seen as a single organization split for convenience at 16. Close liaison between the two phases was as natural an aspiration as links between primary and secondary schools. There are, however, two crucial differences. At 11+ pupils have no alternative, within the state system, but to progress from primary to secondary school. At 16+, on the contrary, education becomes voluntary and there are a variety of options available. Even 11-18 schools have to accept that there are alternatives to automatic progression to their own sixth forms. In some areas where there is mixed provision, the policy is one of choice between the sixth form of an 11-18 school, further education and a sixth form college. There may be available several sixth form and technical colleges, as well as specialist courses in art, music or catering at colleges further afield. Fifth form pupils and their parents must be given equal access to information and advice about each. There will be no 'most favoured nation' clause applied to the sixth form college. Indeed, the relations between colleges and school may sometimes be cool. There may be suspicion of a sixth form college with a high proportion of A level work, resentment of its apparently favourable staffing and escape from discipline problems. This may result in polite disregard for the views of its link tutors. On the college side, there may be the feeling that A level is not fully understood and that the more academic student has some leeway to catch up. Effective collaboration depends on admitting such factors and facing them frankly, on goodwill and informed consultation rather than on elaborate machinery. There are a number of decisions taken in the contributory schools which crucially affect the work of the sixth form college, yet to which it has no prescriptive right to contribute. These include the choice of examining boards, selection of mathematics and science syllabuses, the availability of second and third languages, and policy about entry to O level and CSE.

There are, however, a further series of problems which may not even reach the agenda. What, for example, are the styles of learning which characterize the pupils' experience up to 16 and what influence should these have on the work of the college? Some schools have stressed resource-based learning, choosing syllabuses to facilitate this, while others prefer a traditional emphasis. One school may have adopted mixed ability teaching, another prefers banding, setting or even streaming. Yet at the college all must acclimatize in a short period to a common approach, which inevitably suits some better than others. A school's moral, social and careers education programme may be ambitious, its two year course well resourced and attractively presented. Another school is less ambitious, omitting some elements altogether. If the college provides in its general education programme a compulsory course, the response of some will inevitably be 'we've done it'—applied to sex, marriage, drugs and careers alike! The remedial education in some schools is comprehensive, with careful records available to the college on transfer. In the case of students from other schools it may be weeks before learning difficulties are diagnosed. Able students may well be candidates for entrance to Oxford or Cambridge in their fourth term in the college. They may have been identified in the fifth form and offered enrichment in their likely main subjects, and their promise reported to the college. In other cases, a term may elapse before such high fliers are located and offered the more demanding reading and special help they need. Records transferred as a matter of policy at eleven are frequently not transferred at all at sixteen, sometimes on the grounds that education is now voluntary and the student deserves a fresh start.

It would be absurd to suggest standardization between contributory schools, which may number up to a dozen. What is more, many colleges receive a substantial number of entrants from outside the catchment area and from independent schools. On the other hand, these issues should at least be on the agenda, since the recognition of dissimilarities is itself a contribution to closing the gap. The college and the schools might agree that before embarking on a major curriculum change, there should be discussion by heads and principals, as well as by the appropriate departmental heads. Heads of departments should be aware of developments in each other's sphere. Recent reports on the curriculum from DES, HMI and the Schools Council have been chiefly concerned with the 11–16 age group, while *A Basis for Choice* and the Macfarlane Report concern mainly 16–19 year olds. Both schools and colleges should, however, be aware that many of the issues discussed are inter-related.

In the early 1970's there was much talk of joint appointments to, and exchanges between, the staff of college and school. Little has come of these, largely because they are easier to conceive than to bring to birth. Timetables are inflexible, while continuity of teaching is paramount and autonomy highly prized. In a few places, minority subjects are taught for pupils gathered after school into the college. Peter Symonds College, Winchester, offers Latin to its contributory schools as a two year course to O level and this has been highly successful in generating viable A level teaching groups as well as providing O level Latin for intending linguists and historians. South East Essex S.F. College provides Russian and Latin classes on Saturday morning and further mathematics teaching in several of the 11-16 schools. Colleges often provide emergency support for schools faced with the departure or sickness of specialist staff at a crucial time.

The machinery for liaison between the college and its contributory

A model for liaison between schools and colleges providing post-16 education

1	Heads and principals — Monthly or twice termly meeting
	Exchange of information between schools and college — brochures, examination results, destination of leavers, statistics of university and college entrants. Oversight of liaison and transfer procedure including references, interviews, pupil records. Policy on general education — religious and moral, careers, health, political education. Discussion of learning styles — provision for slow learners and high flyers, banding and setting. Receiving reports from heads of departments and discussion of major curriculum changes. Exchange of information about pastoral care systems.
2	Heads of departments — Termly or half yearly meeting
	Minutes go to heads and principals meeting. Recommendations for in-service training days and occasional conferences of departmental staff. Discussion of curriculum in schools and colleges and problems of transfer at 16. Current issues facing the subject and implications for pre- and post-16 education. Review of examination boards and existing policy. Regular exchange of departmental syllabuses. Occasional meeting of chairmen of heads of departments meetings with heads and principals.
3	The link tutor
	Regular liaison with heads of contributory schools, heads of house, head of upper school, year tutor and head of careers, as appropriate. Initial introduction to parents and pupils at third form parents' meeting before options. When appropriate, advice on foreign languages, sciences, etc. in close collaboration with the school. Attend careers meetings and conventions. Early in fifth form year, general talks to group as part of the school's career programme. Information on life at college helped by students from previous year. Arrange for distribution of college brochure. Individual discussion about course and subject choices involving departmental staff of school and college by arrangement. Follow up queries which arise at interview. Provide school with names of pupils who have entered the college and check that information has been passed on about illnesses, learning difficulties, etc. Provide school with information about former pupils including examination results, jobs they have entered, degree results. *Note* The link tutor works in close collaboration with his or her equivalent in the further education college.

schools is usually on three levels. There are meetings between heads and principal, sometimes including the principal of the technical college and the area education officer. Second, curriculum links are maintained by a meeting of heads of departments of each subject termly or half yearly. Third, there is liaison between individual schools and the college, usually through vice-principal or senior tutors allotted to each school.

Admission and induction

The admission procedure for a sixth form college, like that for a university or polytechnic, is a year round routine. No sooner have new students arrived than next year's admission brochure is rolling off the press into the hands of waiting fifth formers and their parents. If the 1980 Education Act details the information which secondary schools must provide for intending parents, there is no such problem for the sixth form college. Rather the opposite, the problem is to know what to omit in order to contain the document within reasonable compass and how to phase the information so that too much is not provided too early. There are as many procedures as there are colleges. Time scale and methods depend on local circumstances. There are, however, three broad phases into which the procedure can be divided.

1 Information and advice—October to January
There are, at this stage, two main thrusts. First, it is necessary to provide background information about the college—its philosophy, aims and style—so that pupils have an idea of what sort of life they will be leading if they choose to enter the college. Second, the college must provide an introduction to its curriculum, explain what courses it offers and what subjects are available. The temptation is to provide too much information. There is the vexed question of how much should be conveyed in the brochure, how much verbally and how much through a visit to the college. There is a place for each, but the balance between them needs to be carefully adjusted. Brochures may approach university prospectuses in complexity and in appeal to the sophisticated and the able. The bigger problem is to reach the less articulate and the less motivated. Some colleges have set out to produce a brochure with a human face, straightforward text supported by photographs and line drawings, bringing the abstractions of course requirements, syllabus content and career needs down to earth. West Park College, Warley, includes brief biographies of students with their initial qualifications, showing the subjects they chose in the college and what happened when they left—one to enter the police, another to a deck cadetship with Canadian Pacific Steamships and a third to take a degree in Industrial Design at Birmingham Polytechnic. Alton College uses a similar method: 'Peter had narrowly missed gaining O levels and CSE equivalents at his previous school. He was anxious to

enter the Navy at 17 as an apprentice. To gain acceptance he successfully studied English, mathematics and physics at O level and obtained CSE grade 3 in geography and craft technology.' The Alton prospectus provides a further human touch by its biographies of both staff and governors. Skelmersdale College brochure is outstanding in its layout and clarity, and its success in achieving simplicity without being patronizing.

An all-purpose brochure with full information about the college and each subject department will be costly to produce and much of its content will be superfluous to many readers. Some colleges prefer a brochure which offers an outline of the subjects and syllabuses available, supplemented by departmental guides. Fuller information is available from link tutors when the choice of subject has been narrowed to four or five.

In addition to written information, the college will be introduced at this stage by visits, available to pupils during the day and to parents in the evening. This may include a brief address by the principal, an opportunity to see round the college and talk to departmental staff. At the same time careers staff in the schools will be introducing all the opportunites at 16+, and other colleges will be offering their brochures and visits. It is essential that there should be close collaboration between the colleges involved so that the danger of over-exposure and what may appear to be ill-disguised propaganda by rival institutions can be avoided. Responsible restraint will become all the more important when falling rolls begin to reach the age group in the mid-1980's.

2 *Application and acceptance—February to May*
Early in the spring term pupils complete application forms, frequently for more than one post-16 college and sometimes for jobs and apprenticeships, too. Schools usually collect applications and forward them to the college, together with a reference, by half term in February. The reference may be an all purpose one, devised to meet the needs of employers as well as the college, a necessary economy but with consequences that are not wholly satisfactory to the college. There will be a confidential estimate of pupils' likely performance in forthcoming examinations as well as of their motivation and suitability for the course and subjects for which they have applied.

The interview may take place in the college or at school. Some colleges, supported by their schools, see this as an important step to adulthood, comparable with a job interview, and encourage pupils to come alone to the college. Others see the interview in a counselling perspective, with parents and known staff involved and held in a familiar setting, at school. Some involve only one or two members of the college staff, others a wider group. For some students, whose achievement is high and whose intended course is straightforward, the interview will be brief and provide chiefly a first opportunity to meet college staff officially. For others, whatever their likely achievement the interview may be an important stage in the discovery of the right subject options, an opportunity to explain problems which can arise through a mis-match between career intentions and subject choices. Some interviews may lead to questions about Nuffield physics or the right mathematics syllabus and referral to the college's head of department for specific advice. For yet others, the interview may provide a spur to hard work for essential qualifications, without which the hoped for subjects will remain a mirage.

The main interviewing programme will be complete by the end of the spring term. The college will have a list of prospective students, though a proportion will be double-entered for the technical college or be hoping to get a job. The students will have the offer of a place at the college, though the course will be dependent on examination results. Early in the summer term there may be a further stage when the college asks for a response to its offer of a place. The pupil may decide that he prefers a BEC general course at the technical college or that she prefers to take O level at the sixth form college, rather than a catering course at a further education college. If the decision is for the sixth form college, the registration form will be completed in duplicate, accompanied by passport size photographs and the book deposit, and the college subscription may be paid. A third option will arise if the pupil is still undecided. He or she may hold a place provisionally.

The college has now refined its entry list and will make its timetable accordingly. A constant relationship between the number of initial applicants, the number of places offered and accepted in May and the number of students who are admitted in September is usually assumed. Estimating courses and subjects often requires considerable skill, depending on experience of patterns in different subjects in previous years. Some subjects habitually show a decline from offer to entry, others an equally regular increase. The college builds up its own bank of experience to draw on.

3   Bridging and Induction—June to September

From June to September, students are in a curious no man's land. Few schools now attempt to keep their pupils after the completion of examinations. Many colleges provide an introduction to the college during July with a bridging course lasting between two and five days. This gives students an opportunity to sample up to six subjects, including some with which they have no previous acquaintance, such as psychology or sociology, as well as offering a general introduction to the college's leisure activities, to the student common room and to the tutor group. The disadvantages, however, are apparent. Student motivation is not high, full attendance cannot be guaranteed and there is an all-pervading uncertainty which will not be dispelled until late August. The publication of examination results is followed by re-interviews which take place in the last days of the summer holidays and the opening days of the autumn term. Some colleges operate a phased opening to the term to allow staff to concentrate on this crucial task.

The first fortnight of the term is coming increasingly to be regarded as an induction period, marked out from the rest of the year. The college concentrates on three tasks. First, there is familiarization with the buildings, staff, and curriculum, routines and practices, and student organizations and activities. Second, there will be a review of the student's course with an opportunity to discuss any changes which may seem desirable and to give advice on the selection of the student's general education programme. Third, there will be an emphasis on learning skills, with each department postponing a serious start to syllabus content and providing instead assignments which introduce the methods of study which characterize the subject. During this period, staff and students may wear name labels and there may be an evening when parents can meet their son or daughter's group tutor. This stage, too, will be accompanied by supporting literature. Both parents and students are anxious to learn how the college operates in more detail. When will examinations, assessments, reports and parents' evenings take place? How is private study organized? When will careers interviews be available and how will advice on higher education be handled? Queen Elizabeth S.F. College, Darlington, provides a handbook for parents and students with an alphabetical guide to the college beginning with absence, accidents and activities and ending with smoking and valuables.

The transition from school to college is complete. It is perhaps worth noting that the transition from fifth to sixth form is often more thoroughly structured in a two-tier system than when pupils move from fifth to sixth form in the same school. What may be 'inertia choice' is replaced by a deliberate programme of counselling. During the autumn term, the students will probably return to their schools for a certificate evening and staff, some of whom will have taught them for five years, will be interested in their reactions to the college. Indeed, it is important to remember that they will always be at least as much the school's old pupils as the college's old students. Hereford S.F. College, as part of its commitment to the contributory schools, sends them an annual progress report on each former pupil.

Collaboration with further education

One of the virtues of an educational system with a break at sixteen is that it encourages all who wish to continue in full-time education to make a real choice between alternative courses, styles and institutions. Many authorities now include in their reorganization plans provision for close collaboration between the colleges which offer full-time 16-19 provision. For collaboration to be a day to day reality, however, buildings have to be close enough for easy commuting and preferably on adjoining sites.

There needs to be a common timetable using modules which facilitate interchange of students at breaks, but which does not seriously impede the work of either college. There must be an institutional framework within which problems can be solved, rather than perpetuated. And finally, something for which no administrator can legislate, there need to be good personal relationships and a will to work together between senior staff in the co-operating institutions. It is perhaps not surprising that there are as yet relatively few examples of close collaboration. In Solihull students from the sixth form college can take A level in art, home economics and dress at the College of Technology and there is co-operation over the provision of general studies courses. At St. Austell the sixth form college and the Mid-Cornwall College of Further Education are in adjacent buildings and there is a common timetable. At Hereford, the buildings of the sixth form college and the Herefordshire Technical College are physically linked. The two colleges share a sports hall and the sixth form college uses the technical college restaurant. A level Spanish, psychology and home economics are available at the technical college, and art and design at the College of Art. There is collaboration on admissions with a common format used by both colleges, and provision for referral to a neighbouring college.

It is, however, at Nuneaton, that collaboration has been in existence longest and has been taken furthest. King Edward VI College, one of the few voluntary aided sixth form colleges in the country, and the North Warwickshire College of Technology and Art (NWCTA), came together in 1974 in a federation as Nuneaton Junior College. There is a common timetable with three periods each day, 9–10.45, 11.0–12.30 and 1.45–3.45, and since the colleges are 3/4 mile apart, there is commuting by minibus at morning break. There is a common grid of A level subjects, with King Edward VI College offering the usual sixth form subjects, while NWCTA provides those such as computer science and building construction which require specialist facilities. The only A level subjects available in both colleges are economics, English, mathematics and general studies. NWCTA provides O level subjects, though the sixth form college offers repeat courses in mathematics, English and French, as well as German and Spanish as new subjects. An Elective Studies programme run jointly enables students to mix and use the varied facilities of both colleges; at King Edward VI College these are mostly sporting, and at NWCTA mostly technical. Though NWCTA provides for 1300 full-time students, only about 160 are taking an exclusively A level programme, and of these about 60 take one subject at the sixth form college. King Edward VI College has over 400 A level students, of whom about 60 take one subject at NWCTA. There is a Joint Board of Studies for the two colleges, while an Academic Advisory Panel includes the heads of contributory schools as well as representatives of the careers and advisory service and the area education officer. Application to the college is by joint entry form and the two Directors of Studies work closely together over initial interviewing and over problems which arise when unexpected examination results in O level or CSE involve a change of college. This is no more a blue-print than any other scheme. It does, however, eliminate competition for students in a relatively small town. It facilitates joint use of resources and staff as well as buildings, and it enlarges the opportunities which each college can offer its students.

The Nuneaton Junior College is a federation of two colleges. The Cambridge Collegiate Board, on the other hand, is a means of rationalizing entry to six centres, each providing a variety of opportunities for full-time 16–19 education in the city and the surrounding country. It is reminiscent of a small-scale UCCA. There are two sixth form colleges, Hills Road and Long Road, each catering for about 500 students, and two 11–18 schools, Impington Village College with 120 in the sixth form, and Netherhall School, with 180. In addition to the College of Further Education there is the Cambridgeshire College of Arts and Technology with 2000 full-time students of whom 700 are following degree courses. Open evenings are held at each centre in the early autumn. Applications are received between December and February by the Secretary of the Collegiate Board, a full-time officer based in the city. Applications are then sent to the centre of first choice which interviews candidates and offers either a firm place or more likely, one conditional on appropriate examination results. If the centre is unable to offer a place, the application is sent to the second choice school or college. The final stage takes place in late August and early September when the Collegiate Board operates a clearing house for unplaced applicants. Parents and students are interviewed, though no responsibility is accepted for students who have departed on holiday as the crucial time approaches. The system is an effective rationalization of what could otherwise be an unwieldy multi-application process. Its end product is predictable; a high proportion of academic A level students seek and obtain a place at one of the sixth form colleges.

That distance need not be a bar to collaboration is shown by the scheme in operation in the Castle Point and Rochford area of Essex. Here, institutions seven miles apart, South East Essex S.F. College and technical colleges at Southend and Thurrock, have a joint prospectus of courses. An area course advisory officer, who is a vice-principal at the sixth form college, is link tutor between the schools and the colleges. Parents' evenings are held in each school on two consecutive evenings (one for A level and another for one year courses), at which all the colleges are represented.

8

The student view

Student expectations

The Schools Council Sixth Form Survey was undertaken in 1967**(31)**. This was just too early to include a sixth form college in its sample of 154 institutions providing full-time education for the age group. It did, however, indicate an awareness on the part of heads and staffs of a change which was coming over the attitude of sixth formers to their schools. They expected to be given greater freedom and they were more critical of paternalistic authority than they had been ten years before. They had wider interests outside the school and less dependence upon it for their social and sporting life. The jobs they now undertook, at weekends and in the holidays, conferred a greater awareness of the natural constraints of adult society and impatience with what they took to be the artificial restraints of school. The boundaries deliberately marked out by the traditional sixth form, separating it from the world outside, were trampled down. There was less acceptance of the role of exemplar to younger pupils. Yet sixth formers were at the same time more aware that they needed the qualifications for higher education and careers which the sixth form had to confer. Staff surveyed appeared on balance to approve the greater independence shown by older pupils and even to welcome the critical appraisal to which sixth form life was treated.

Though the sixth form college was not a deliberate response to such needs, it is nevertheless the legatee of many of the attitudes which were then becoming evident. One of its major advantages is that it can deliberately set out to create an environment which meets the specific needs of this transitional age-group.

There is, however, still a degree of impatience expressed by many sixth form college students at the contrast between their expectation of the life style they will be offered and the reality of college life as they experience it. This has often been fed, quite unconsciously, by staff at the comprehensive school who have, during the fifth form year, held out the college as the goal which will offer the freedom they aspire to but which they cannot yet be granted. The sixth form college, in its promotional literature and through liaison tutors may, equally unintentionally, have created similar expectations. It is after all not easy to explain how daily life in the college will be different, without erecting an ideal which may in the cold light of day not be fully realizable. It is still harder to articulate a difference of philosophy which distinguishes the approach of the college from that of the school. Students expect to achieve adult status during the summer holiday between school and college, like butterflies emerging from the chrysalis in the sunshine. There is no word which more completely encapsulates the expectation and the disappointment than 'adult'. 'The college doesn't treat us as adults', can mean no more than that students still have to attend lessons and hand in written work, that smoking is frowned upon and reports are provided for parents. It may of course also indicate that the college has not achieved the right balance between imposed discipline and self-discipline or has not been seen by the students to do so. The college is aware that the summer holiday does not bring a metamorphosis, that the change in status from school to adulthood is a gradual one and that it would be abdicating responsibility if it were to behave as though its students were undergraduates. Student impatience at the slow change of status and staff impatience at extravagant student demands would be one way of analysing the tension sometimes to be found in the college.

The student's view, though it may lack objectivity, provides an important perspective, and this chapter is concerned with an attempt to see the college through the eyes of its members. A survey *A Student's View of a Sixth Form College* was circulated in the summer term of 1981 in seven colleges, two in the North of England, two in the Midlands and three in the South of England. Numbers in the colleges varied from 250 to over 1000. They included urban, rural and suburban colleges. Their designation as sixth form colleges took place between 1970 and 1977. A total of 1500 students completed the questionnaire. The results were scaled to give approximately equal weighting to each college. The questionnaire referred to subsequently as *A Student's View* has been used as part of the evidence of the attitude taken by students to their experience in a sixth form college. In many ways it confirms conclusions reached by Dean and Choppin in their much wider survey**(11)**.

Settling down and making friends

> *It does not allow time to settle down properly as you are only there for two years ... At your previous school you are already settled in and the teachers know your capabilities.*

> *After going to a small girls' school the college has provided a chance for me to break away from a very sheltered environment and learn how to mix more easily.*

Criticism of sixth form colleges has stressed the dislocation to the education of a sixteen year old caused by the need to adapt to a new institution, particularly for those whose course will last only nine months. It would be facile to dismiss the criticism altogether. Transition from school to college needs to be handled sensitively and with expertise if the break is to have no deleterious effects. At the same time a new experience can be valuable, and for the one year student the opportunity for a gentle transition at sixteen can be an important preparation for the move to work at seventeen. For the student from a single sex school, whether day or boarding, the transition is frequently a valuable contribution to general education.

	% Girls	% Boys
I felt at home from the very beginning.	17	20
I settled down in a few days.	35	41
I settled down in a few weeks.	31	24
I settled down after about a term.	11	10
I never really settled down.	6	5

Boys, it appears, settle down rather more easily than girls, but a few take a substantial period to settle: 15% a term or more. 'Feeling at home' was not defined, but it might include familiarity with the college buildings and facilities, awareness of the routine, and knowing whom to consult about a change of subject, how to join a society or play badminton, where to spend private study and how to take a book out of the library. The subtler part is the creation of relationships with staff and other students. The Schools Council Survey found that it was heads and staff who were most aware of the problem of transition to the sixth form, while students took the change for granted. The sixth form colleges may have reversed this. Students are aware of the novelty of the institution they have entered, while staff tend to take it for granted, underrating the need for a structured and deliberate period of induction for students who have known neither each other nor the college before.

	% Girls			% Boys		
	Yes	No	Don't know	Yes	No	Don't know
I really feel I belong to the college.	54	20	27	45	24	31
Most of my friends are at the college.	60	37	3	69	27	4
I have made new friends at the college.	97	1	2	98	1	1

A 'sense of belonging' is much harder to define. Some students, particularly girls, going from a school to a sixth form college, are aware of a 'lost sense of tradition'. On the other hand, the smaller colleges and those with fewer contributory schools have some advantage in creating a sense of belonging. Friendships within the college, both old and new, flourish. One year students are rather more likely to find their friends have gone to a technical college or to work than to the college and girls find that rather fewer of their friends have accompanied them to college. The making of new friends is a universal experience and one which, in view of the large catchment area and the social diversity of most colleges, enlarges the student's horizons substantially. A regular stream of eighteenth birthday parties characterizes the social life of the second year students.

Getting to know staff, particularly in a large college, is not easy but then nor is it in a large comprehensive school. Only about one third of the students felt that they knew all the staff and this figure fell to one sixth in the largest college with a staff of over eighty. Relations between staff and student are good; 80% characterized relations as 'friendly'.

The academic programme

Students enter the college primarily with the intention of acquiring academic qualifications. The intrinsic value of further education, the opportunity to broaden their horizons, a natural interest in particular academic subjects or even peer group or parental pressure, are all minor considerations. Success involves learning how to work independently and acquiring the methods of work appropriate to the subject being studied. The contribution of the college is to encourage the effective use of private study and to provide an atmosphere which is both sufficiently structured and free enough to encourage initiative and experiment. *A Student's View* found that 80% of girls and 70% of boys thought they had about the right amount of private study time, while 13% of girls and 20% of boys would have liked more. Behind the question is the very much bigger one of learning how to use the time allocated: *You get no tuition about the best ways to use private study. Having not had any previously I first saw it as a good skive. I now regret it.*

Many were aware that private study was a novelty, 'a perk', 'a lark', and only after a substantial amount of time had been wasted did they learn how to make some use of it. The demand for advice on how to use private study came both from colleges where there was a compulsory framework and those where there was greater freedom. The problem is evidently what to do and how to do it, rather than where to do it and under whose supervision. Work assignments at home, too, presented problems. Required to produce an essay tomorrow, the fifth former will usually comply. A request to the new sixth former to hand in an essay in ten days induces either procrastination or anxiety about meeting the deadline. Students need guidance about how to allocate time between work, leisure and their family, how to be fair to the demands of different subjects in their timetable and how to undertake preparatory work for an essay or a longer assignment. *A Student's View* showed students asking for advice on note taking in class and from books, for tests to enable them to consolidate knowledge, for essays to be frankly assessed and for work schemes for half a term or more in advance.

> *I can work better in a stricter atmosphere.*
>
> *I wish the teachers were more strict when they asked for work.*
>
> *In the first year homework should be stressed more and possibly made compulsory.*
>
> *Because of the amount of freedom many people seem not to take work seriously and, since they have to be in the college, people who do not work are socially separate from the rest of the college all the time.*

If the use of private study and learning skills can be taught either by a special course or as part of the responsibility of each subject department, the general atmosphere in the college is a matter for discussion by staff. Students evidently prefer an environment which has a degree of astringency, even though there may be criticism, at least from a vocal minority, of the restrictions involved. A permissive approach to homework makes it harder to keep to deadlines, while the conscientious student likes to feel that his or her zeal is regarded as the norm.

> *Forcing me to learn is the only way with someone afflicted, as I am, with laziness and aversion to work.*
>
> *Threatening to throw me out would have got me down to some work.*

Here is the demand of students who, at the end of the course, realize that freedom is something they have been unable to handle and that in retrospect at least they would have preferred a coercive regime. To this demand the answer is pastoral rather than regulative; discussion early in the course about the nature of freedom and the self-discipline it requires. There can be no reversion to threats and punishment.

	% Girls			% Boys		
	Yes	No	Don't know	Yes	No	Don't know
I chose the right subjects.	66	24	10	65	26	9
I wish I had chosen at least one subject differently.	43	53	4	45	50	5
I wish I had received more advice before choosing my college subjects.	44	47	9	42	49	9

The choice of subjects is both crucial and difficult in a sixth form college. There is a bewildering multiplicity of subjects and alternative syllabuses available, while staff who will be teaching them are not normally available for detailed counselling before the beginning of the September term. There will, of course, always be students whose reaction to difficulty or failure in a subject is to believe that an alternative subject would have proved easier or more congenial, or whose friends aver that another subject is better taught. Some dissatisfaction will occur in any institution. There is, however, evidence from *A Student's View* that more care needs to be devoted to subject choice both before students enter the college and during the induction period in September.

Dean, Bradley et al. reported antipathy to the whole idea of general studies shown by some sixth form students, whether or not there was freedom of choice within the course**(10)**. *A Student's View* presents a rather more complex picture. 32% of girls and 40% of boys thought general studies was a waste of time. In some colleges this view was held very much more widely. The reaction is more favourable when the general studies referred to includes games and recreational courses, while those where disillusionment or apathy is strongest are those where courses are compulsory or chiefly academic. Most colleges would probably concede that their own convictions about the value of general studies are not matched by student enthusiasm. Courses with a popular appeal such as 'The Economics of Everyday Life' take precedence over artistic appreciation or ethical discussion. It may be some consolation to staff battling against apathy to realize that the student who apparently conforms to the stereotype of disapproval of general studies may in ten years proclaim that a life long love of industrial archaeology or Renaissance painting began at college. This is what one college principal describes as 'the fallacy of instant response', a factor of which all curriculum planners should be aware.

Rules and sanctions

> *There are very few rules here—not enough in my opinion.*
>
> *As far as rules are concerned, I think you know what is expected of you when you enter a sixth form college. If you want more freedom, then a technical college would probably suit you better.*
>
> *All rules are unnecessary since we are here by choice.*

Some students enter college believing that rules belong to the world of school which they have left two months previously. Entry to college is seen as a change of status and one which ideally would be symbolized by freedom from 'petty restrictions', which means any rule whose justification is not immediately self-evident. Rules, however, though fewer than in the secondary school and as far as possible justified by reason and common sense, are a characteristic of sixth form colleges as they are of any other human institution. Rules are part of the responsibility exercised by adults in creating an appropriate environment for the education of adolescents. No amount of student pressure justifies the withdrawal of adult control or the failure to enforce the rules which have been made. Indeed, the capacity to resist student pressure in a reasonable and good humoured way is an important part of the hidden curriculum of the college. Some students define freedom as the right to be unfettered by rules. This is, however, negative freedom. Far more important is the positive understanding of freedom, the purpose of which is to make opportunities more accessible and right choices easier. Students, for example, often demand the right to stay away from college when they have no taught lessons. To concede this, particularly at the beginning of the college course, may in practice prevent the less motivated student from learning to use the college library, making new friendships, discussing work with staff in a free period, or joining a voluntary cookery course—all in fact restricting their positive freedom in the interests of theoretical absence of restraint.

	% Girls			% Boys		
	Yes	No	Don't know	Yes	No	Don't know
The rules of the college are about right.	72	18	10	64	27	9
You are given too much freedom.	4	95	1	5	92	3
There are too many rules and restrictions.	26	65	9	28	64	8
The college treats you like an adult.	42	38	20	49	35	16

It is sometimes too relaxed. I feel I cannnot work in a too relaxed atmosphere, but then again not in a too rigid one either.

A *Student's View* contained four overlapping questions about freedom, rules and adult status. There were significant differences between the seven colleges. Those in the North of England and the Midlands accepted the rules more readily and were more likely to feel that they enjoyed adult status than those in the South of England. Girls showed greater acceptance of rules than boys.

There was a further question inviting respondents to indicate any rule they resented or felt to be unnecessary. One issue dominated all others in all colleges and was mentioned by about 80% of all those who chose to respond to the question, that of compulsory attendance. It occurred in a variety of guises according to the rules of the particular college. For some, it was resentment at 9 a.m. registration if they were not due at a lesson immediately afterwards. For others, the issue was the right to leave college during the day when they were not being taught. If this was conceded by the college after a certain time, then there was pressure that the time should be earlier or the restriction lifted altogether. If the college held an afternoon registration at 2 p.m., but then allowed students to leave, there was a demand that registration should be at 12.30. Some students focused their resentment on any requirement to spend private study in any particular place or under any supervision. If colleges do retain the requirement of full-time attendance they clearly need to define its rationale to students and then to enforce it. 'It is too easy to miss lessons', was not an isolated comment, though it is not one which is likely to be heard except through the anonymity of a questionnaire.

A second category of rule which is likely to provoke restraint is one which students see as a continuation of school status. Assembly, even if it is disguised by the title College Meeting, is not readily accepted as a necessity particularly first thing in the morning. Few students appear to have enjoyed assembly at school and even if imaginatively led it still has paternalistic overtones. Some students, however, will readily admit the problem that if the college never meets it is unlikely to retain a sense of corporate identity. Tutorial periods, the requirement to produce an absence note (whether it is written by the student or by a parent), and to return reply slips from letters to parents, are all matters which may provoke a less than enthusiastic response.

The social conventions of the college are seen by some students to be restrictive. Drinking during the lunchtime, once the students reach eighteen, appears to them to be a decision which they should take for themselves. Rules about smoking and gambling on the premises are noted, too, as unnecessary restrictions by the more vocal. Finally, colleges which have dress regulations find that students are unable to discern the rationale behind them. A number of colleges suggest that the model is what is appropriate for work in an office. The students are unable to understand and the college has to explain why the office is chosen rather than the building site or the polytechnic, when both are just as likely subsequent destinations as the office.

A student view of the sixth form college

Going to a sixth form college gives a student a really clean start to a maturer life. There is a chance to turn over a new leaf, when perhaps you've had a disastrous school life.

You need a great deal of self-discipline.

I have enjoyed my stay at the college, made new friends, learnt new things and personally it has been one of the best things I've ever done.

I find the general student body apathetic and unwilling to make the most of the college facilities.

I have never really enjoyed myself here, but then I am not really a good example as I resented the fact that I couldn't get a job and had to come to college anyway. I came here thinking it was going to be just like school (which I didn't like either) and it was.

There is a very congenial atmosphere in the college which is conducive to general enjoyment but the existence of lessons and work does get in the way!

I enjoyed every minute of it.

There is of course no such thing as a student view of the sixth form college, nor even general agreement about any one college. Students in the same college may share similar experiences—be in the same tutor group and teaching sets and participate in similar recreational activities—but respond to the college in wholly different ways. One will find lessons tedious, the rules irritating, the social life tame and expectations disappointed. Another will settle down quickly, enjoy lessons, find congenial social activities, help to edit the magazine, join the student council and find the whole experience stimulating.

In a school system with a break at sixteen:	% Girls	% Boys
Sixth formers gain through not being with younger pupils.	76	74
Sixth formers lose through not being with younger pupils.	14	7
Younger pupils gain through there being no sixth form.	24	23
Younger pupils lose through there being no sixth form.	32	26

Rather more girls than boys felt they had lost through not being with younger pupils, while about a quarter felt that younger pupils gained and another quarter that they lost through being in a school with no sixth form.

What I have gained from the college. Tick as many of the following as you like:

	% Girls	% Boys
Extra qualifications (I hope)	97	95
New friends	93	93
An enjoyable year or two years	60	66
Greater maturity	58	51
Learnt how to work on my own	48	45

When the Schools Council Survey attempted to define what it was, apart from examination success, that students gained from a sixth form course, it found that it was greater maturity, responsibility and independence which were named most frequently and that it was students who had been prefects, house captains, society officers or committee members who were most aware of increased maturity. *A Student's View* produced a different set of outcomes. Students were agreed that they had obtained qualifications and made new friends. Awareness of greater maturity was only mentioned by just over half of all students. An awareness of maturity, it appears, though not necessarily the maturity itself, may result from the contrast between the third or fourth former in the school and the person the sixth former knows he or she has now become. It may arise from minority status, enjoying a special relationship with staff and running activities for younger children. The maturity which resulted from prefectship was itself sometimes spurious or precocious and its disappearance need not in general be regretted. Dr David Newsome has pointed out that the nineteenth century public school could produce men who had never been boys as well as boys who never became men. The figure for 'an enjoyable year or two years' may appear lower than expected. It is easily forgotten that adolescents, though appearing self-confident and easy going, are often insecure and tense. They find relations with their own and the opposite sex not always a happy experience. These are years in which relations with parents can be turbulent, while the academic pressure of the college is by no means congenial to all those who undergo it.

	% Girls	% Boys
I am pleased I came to the college.	81	86
I should have preferred a technical college.	5	3
I should have preferred to stay in a sixth form at my previous school.	9	7
I wish I had left school altogether at sixteen.	5	4

The impression gleaned from *A Student's View* was overwhelmingly one of pleasure at having come to college. Relatively few, even in retrospect and even in colleges which had been recently reorganized, would have preferred an alternative course of action at sixteen. It is hard to escape the conclusion that the sixth form college, born as is the way with many English institutions, of accident, expediency and pragmatism, has turned out to be highly successful as a means of providing full-time education for the 16–19 age group.

9
Conclusion

The sixth form college is both old and new, both achievement and aspiration. Its roots lie in the development in schools of provision for the 16 to 19 age group, at first chiefly academic, recently for an altogether wider target group. Its life span is as yet brief: relatively few colleges have existed for more than five years fully developed and catering exclusively for the age group. The majority of the first generation of sixth form colleges evolved from grammar schools and only gradually became comprehensive in curriculum and ethos. In this respect, the newly created colleges had an easier task. The colleges of the second generation are likely, for the most part, to result from the reorganization of comprehensive schools as a consequence of falling rolls. They will from the beginning be comprehensive colleges and will be designed to take their place alongside further education colleges in providing for the needs of the 16 to 19 age group.

The plans announced by Birmingham may well set a pattern. Between 1983 and 1986 this large metropolitan borough proposes to open seven colleges with an average size of 700 (dropping by 1993 to 500). Though they will replace the authority's sixth forms and be organized according to Schools Regulations, they will not be called sixth form colleges. They will be designated by locality alone, indistinguishable by title from the seven further education colleges. There will, from the beginning, be close collaboration between the further education colleges and the new colleges, in provision of courses both locally and across the city. Birmingham illustrates the direction which change in the 1980's may take more widely. Unification of Schools and F.E. Regulations, however, will be essential if close collaboration, including interchange of staff between the two sectors, is to be achieved. Yet this is a task of daunting complexity. Each sector values both its own tradition and its connections with other parts of the education system. Sixth form colleges have grown up as part of the secondary school system, while further education colleges have links with advanced further and higher education. Any coming together in the 16–19 sector will inevitably affect the ethos of the sixth form college, not necessarily in directions which all will approve.

In the meantime there will be increasing collaboration between sixth form colleges and their neighbours in further education. Courses will be planned in co-operation to avoid overlap and wasteful competition. Already, joint approaches to contributory schools, with link tutors working closely together and co-ordinated interviewing arrangements, are being developed. Where colleges are close to each other the specialist facilities of each will be made available to the other and a common timetable matrix will be adopted. In some areas a tertiary college may be a logical development. Sheffield is one large authority which is planning tertiary colleges for the whole city. Alton college, a purpose-built sixth form college in a small Hampshire town, has been designated as a tertiary college from 1983, to enable it to offer wider courses and to provide for part-time and adult students in the area.

There will be changes inside the sixth form colleges to meet the needs of the 1980's. More students, faced with the prospect of unemployment and with the need for higher qualifications to compete in the job market, are already entering the college to take a one year course. Some courses, which have hitherto been completed in one year, may in future be planned to last two years. Such courses might be of a sandwich type, allowing periods of work experience alternating with the examination course. Other students may enter the college for a planned three year course, concentrating in the first year on one A level subject alongside further O level subjects, before taking up two further A levels in the second year. Profile reporting is likely to be adopted alongside examinations at 17+ and 18+, while the pre-vocational emphasis suggested in *A Basis for Choice* will influence the course structure of all students in the college.

In the aftermath of the failure of the N and F proposals there is concern at the narrow and specialized curriculum which is the staple diet of many sixth formers. A new initiative to break the stranglehold of the three subject A level might come from sixth form colleges, perhaps along the lines of the International Baccalaureate. In the meantime the growth of general studies examinations at A level, O level and CEE, making use of a variety of imaginative syllabuses, is making a valuable contribution to general education.

Curriculum and pastoral care are increasingly seen as two sides of the same coin. With the college staff likely in the conditions of the 1980's to remain stable, there may be opportunities for an exchange of role between senior tutor and head of department, for instance, which would enrich the experience of both. Subject tutor and group tutor are two aspects of the same job, with an overall concern for the student's academic progress and general welfare in the college. Group tutors are increasingly involved in the counselling which takes place when students enter the college and, once involved, the tutor's interest is likely to grow. Careers education and learning and life skills courses are becoming more important aspects of the college's work, and in each the group tutor has an important part to play.

As they contemplated the first sixth form college and foresaw the possibilities of the new institution, the staff of Luton Technical School referred to 'this fascinating experiment in sixth form living'. The sixth form colleges have, in their first sixteen years, proved their ability to fulfil this aspiration. In the 1980's sixth form colleges are no longer an experiment but an accomplished fact. They offer an educational opportunity and experience which will be shared by a steadily increasing proportion of the 16-19 age group.

Note: The Birmingham plans referred to on page 99 were withdrawn by the Local Education Authority in May 1982. A scheme including three sixth form colleges has since been substituted. The point, however, remains that future years are likely to see both a lessening of the distinction between sixth form and further education colleges, and closer collaboration between the two types of institution.

References and bibliography

1. Association of Principals of Sixth Form Colleges. *Organisation of Sixth Form Colleges*, APVIC, 1981. (Circulated to members)
2. Benn, C. and Simon, B. *Half Way There*, second edition, Penguin Books, 1972.
3. Bowen, W. E. and others. *Vision of a Sixth Form College*, Secondary Technical School, Luton, 1965.
4. Carter, D. 'Reflections on a Sixth Form College', in *Journal of the Assistant Masters Association*, December 1970.
5. Case, R. 'A college certificate course for less able students', in *Wessex Studies in Special Education*, King Alfred's College, Winchester, 1981.
6. Central Advisory Council for Education. *15–18* (The Crowther Report), HMSO, 1959.
7. Christie, T. and Oliver, R. 'Academic performance at age 18-plus as related to school organisation', *Research in Education*, 1969:2, Manchester University Press, 1969.
8. City and Guilds of London Institute. *Foundation for a Career*, 1978.
9. Councils and Education Press. *The Sixth Form College in Practice*, Councils and Education Press, 1972.
10. Dean, J., Bradley, K., Choppin, B. and Vincent, D. *The Sixth Form and its Alternatives*, NFER, 1979.
11. Dean, J. and Choppin, B. *Educational Provision 16–19*, NFER, 1977.
12. DES. *Curriculum 11–16*, HMSO, 1977.
13. DES. *Examinations 16–18 a consultative paper*, DES, 1980.
14. DES. *The Legal Basis of Further Education*, DES, 1981.
15. Edwards, A. D. *The Changing Sixth Form in the Twentieth Century*, Routledge and Kegan Paul, 1970.

Further Education Curriculum Review and Development Unit
16. *A Basis for Choice*, FECRDU, 1979.
17. *ABC in Action*, FECRDU, 1981.
18. *Signposts: a map of 16–19 educational provision*, FECRDU, 1980.

19. General Studies Association. *The Curriculum of the Open Sixth*, GSA, 1976.
20. Hampshire Education Authority. *Paths to Understanding*, a handbook to Religious Education in Hampshire Schools, Hampshire County Council, 1980.

21 Headmasters' Association. *Providing for a Sixth Form College*, HMA, 1977.
22 HMSO. *Proposals for a Certificate of Extended Education* (The Keohane Report), HMSO, 1979.
23 HMSO. *Education for 16–19 Year Olds* (The Macfarlane Report), HMSO, 1980.
24 Holt, M. *The Tertiary Sector*, Hodder and Stoughton, 1980.
25 International Baccalaureate Office. *General Guide to the International Baccalaureate*, IBO, 1972 and later editions.
26 International Baccalaureate Office. *Theory of Knowledge Course*. Syllabus and Teaching Notes. Aston Educational Monographs Number 2, IBO, 1976.
27 Janes, F. and Miles, J. C. (Eds.). *Tertiary Colleges*, 1979. Bridgwater College.
28 King, R. *School and College*, Routledge and Kegan Paul, 1976.
29 King, R. Wearing. *The English Sixth Form College*, Pergamon, 1968.
30 Macfarlane, E. *Sixth Form Colleges*, Heinemann, 1978.
31 Martin-Williams, R., Raven, J. and Ritchie, J. *Sixth Form Pupils and Teachers*, Volume 1, Books for Schools for the Schools Council, 1970.
32 Pedley, R., *The Comprehensive School*. Pelican, 1963.
33 Peterson, A. D. C. *The Future of the Sixth Form*, Routledge and Kegan Paul, 1973.
34 Rutter, M., Maughan, B., Mortimore, P. and Ouston, J. *Fifteen Thousand Hours*, Open Books, 1979.

Schools Council
35 Examinations Bulletin Number 38 *Examinations at 18-plus, resource implications of an N and F curriculum*, Evans Methuen Educational, 1978.
36 Working Paper Number 5 *Sixth Form Curriculum and Examinations*, HMSO, 1966.
37 Working Paper Number 45 *16–19 Growth and Response 1. Curricular bases*, Evans Methuen, 1972.
38 Working Paper Number 46 *16–19 Growth and Response 2. Examination structures*, Evans Methuen, 1973.
39 Working Paper Number 47 *Preparation for degree courses*, Evans Methuen, 1973.
40 Working Paper Number 60 *Examinations at 18-plus: the N and F Studies*, Evans Methuen, 1978.

41 Secondary Heads Association. 'Staffing and Curriculum in 11–16 Schools', in *SHA Review*, July, 1979.
42 Secondary Heads Association, *Youth in Need*, SHA, 1982.
43 Spooner, H. *A History of Taunton's School, Southampton 1760–1967*, Southampton, 1968.
44 Standing Conference of Principals of Sixth Form and Tertiary Colleges. *Compendium of Sixth Form and Tertiary Colleges*, First Edition, 1974. Fifth Edition, 1982.

45 Taylor, P., Reid, W. and Holley, B. *The English Sixth Form*, Routledge and Kegan Paul, 1974.
46 Vincent, D. and Dean, J. *One Year Courses in Colleges and Sixth Forms*, NFER, 1979.
47 Stephenson, R. J. 'Personal and academic development of the individual at sixth form level', in *Comprehensive Education, Report of a DES Conference December 1977*, HMSO, 1978.

Further information

The Association of Sixth Form College Principals
 Chairman: A. J. Baker, C.B.E., Brockenhurst College
 Secretary: J. L. Glazier, South East Essex SFC.

The Secondary Heads Association has a Sixth Form Colleges Panel. Information from: The General Secretary, 29 Gordon Square, London WC1H 0PS.

The Compendium of Sixth Form and Tertiary Colleges 1982 can be obtained from A. J. Dobell, Principal of Barnsley Sixth Form College, Huddersfield Road, Barnsley, S75 1DS, price £4.